The Complete Log House Book

The Complete Log House Book

Dale Mann and
Richard Skinulis

Photography by Nancy Shanoff
Illustrations by Jane Nelson

McGraw-Hill Ryerson Limited
Toronto   Montreal   New York   St. Louis
San Francisco   Auckland   Beirut   Bogata
Düsseldorf   Johannesburg   Lisbon   London   Lucerne
Madrid   Mexico   New Delhi   Panama   Paris
San Juan   São Paulo   Singapore   Sydney   Tokyo

The Complete Log House Book

Design by Sharon M. Black

ISBN 0-07-082817-2

1 2 3 4 5 6 7 8 9 10 BP 8 7 6 5 4 3 2 1 0 9

Printed and bound in Canada
by The Bryant Press Limited

Canadian Cataloguing in Publication Data
Mann, Dale, date
   The complete log house book
Bibliography: p.
Includes index.
ISBN 0-07-082817-2

1. Log cabins.   I. Skinulis, Richard, date.
II. Title.

TH4840.M36   694   C79-094482-0

The following sources of photographs are acknowledged:

Algonquin Park Museum Archives: 17 (top right)

Bill Armstrong: 83 (right)

Canadian Pacific: 24, 25

Ken Edwards: 74

Stan Garrod: 26

Glenbow-Alberta Institute, Calgary: 20 (right)

Inventaire des Biens Culturels du Québec: 13 (right)

W. Kenyon, courtesy of the Royal Ontario Museum,
Toronto, Canada: 21 (top)

Dale Mann: 14 (left, center top and bottom), 15, 16
(left), 23 (right), 31, 32, 34 (left), 35, 48, 49 (top and
center), 50, 51, 54 (right), 62, 65, 68, 70, 71 (left), 86,
96, 97, 101 (left), 103, 104, 105, 108, 126, 133 (right),
134, 135, 136, 137, 138, 139, 141, 143, 144, 147, 148
(top and bottom right), 149 (bottom right), 150, 151,
152

Ruth Mann: 71 (right)

Ontario Archives: 17 (left), 18 (top left), 21 (bottom),
22 (lower right), 23 (left)

Parks Canada: 12, 13 (left), 57 (left)

Public Archives Canada: 10, 18 (top and bottom
right), 19, 20 (left), 22 (left), 123

Nancy Shanoff: cover, 14 (left and top right), 16
(right), 28, 34 (right), 36, 42 (left), 43, 44, 46 (left), 47,
49 (bottom), 53, 54 (left), 55 (left), 57 (center and
right), 63, 66, 67, 72, 73, 76, 77, 80, 81, 84, 85, 88,
89, 92, 93, 98, 99, 101 (right), 106, 107, 109, 112,
113, 114, 115, 116, 117, 118, 119, 120, 127, 128
(right), 132, 133, 145, 154, 155 (right), 156, 157, 161

Richard Skinulis: 27, 130 (left), 140 (right), 155 (left)

United Church Archives, Victoria University,
Toronto: 26 (right)

Rob Van Vliet: 128 (left)

Laurie Windsor: 129, 130 (right), 131, 133 (left).

contents

acknowledgments

The first group among the many people we would like to thank for their help in putting this book together are the legions of dedicated builders who built the houses we visited and the hospitable owners who permitted us to photograph them. We had the benefit of the experience of a number of log builders. Bill Armstrong, Dale's partner in the early days of their log building business, helped with the historical and stackwall sections, and provided encouragement just when it was needed. Lydia Vanderstaal (who is seen in the stackwall photograph on page 155) shared with us her knowledge of stackwall construction. Mike Arthur, Ken Edwards, John Gulland and Judy McCallum, a group of latter-day settlers from the Ottawa Valley, gave us the benefit of their experiments in piece-on-piece log building.

We are especially grateful to the three men who make up V.L.H. Log Builders of Killaloe, Ontario: Rob Van Vliet, Lee LaFont and Grant Hooker (seen demonstrating the scribing and V-notching sequence). They all gave freely and generously of their hard-won knowledge which comprised the bulk of the long log and piece-on-piece sections.

An important group of professional log builders we would like to thank are, of course, those who made up Mann and Armstrong and later Dale Mann Ltd., and who built the houses shown on the cover of the book and on pages 72, 73, 77, 85, 98, 106 and 107: Bill Bosward, Jack Cooper, Walter Desroches, Frank Paul, Ron Publow, Bob Stephens, David Strudwick, Len Van Dyk (seen in the dovetail notching sequence) and Peter Williams.

Gil Bartholomew's studies on stackwall construction were a big help to us in writing that section, as was information on various aspects of log building from Jim Cleave of the Ontario Agricultural Museum. Lynn Marriott retyped some of our rough manuscript so it was readable, and Ruth Mann was ready with helpful suggestions and constant support. We would also like to thank Carroll Burritt and Glynn Shannon for taking time from busy schedules to guide us around to some of the houses we photographed, and the people at Anzalone-McLeod studio for their cooperation and support.

We have been fortunate to have in the book Nancy Shanoff's excellent photographs, which capture and record the beauty and variety of the buildings so well, and to have benefited from her general collaboration and strong drive for perfection throughout the project. The essential feeling for log building is conveyed by Jane Nelson's charming and accomplished illustrations.

Finally, we want to thank Jerry Dunnigan, Tommy Dunnigan, George Holly, Lorne O'Connor and Barney Ristau, and other local people from Cormac and the Ottawa Valley, who passed on their log building tradition and made us feel welcome.

D.M.
R.S.

This book was conceived almost two years ago in a tiny room in the Oro Negro Hotel in a village at the headwaters of the Amazon in Equador. Dale and I had been waiting there for three days, trying to get someone to take us down river, and in the steamy tropical heat our minds began to wander back home to the time when we had started working with logs. . . .

We had lived for six years in a rural area that has a long history of log building, the upper Ottawa Valley of eastern Ontario. The farm we bought with some friends had an old log house on it, the first one many of us had ever really seen at close hand. We liked it, and as we expanded out on the land, our friends began buying and dismantling other old log buildings in the area, and putting them together again on the farm. Slowly we learned the terms for strange new tools, how to put the logs up, how to hew new ones, and how to cut the dovetail corners the area is famous for. We realized that here was a lost art that we — and many other people scattered across the continent — were helping to keep alive.

Many of the old log houses in our area had been abandoned and were falling into disrepair. Dale decided to take advantage of the revival of interest in log houses, and began making his living by buying old houses and rebuilding them. During the years that followed, Dale and his associates traveled thousands of miles, chatted and bargained with countless people, and learned a great deal, delving into the arcanum of this important architectural form. In five years, they had reconstructed eight log buildings, and bought and sold many more sets of logs. When they started out, Dale and those who worked with him learned their craft by studying old buildings, by piecing together bits of information from various sources, and by trial and error, since most of the information they needed was not readily available — much of it had been lost with the deaths of the original builders of the last remaining log houses.

The lack of a good, all-round log building book was obvious to us, and Dale decided to enlist my help in writing such a book. We wanted to draw on Dale's special area of knowledge, the reconstruction of hewn log buildings, as well as the experience of others who had begun to build new houses using long log, piece-on-piece and stackwall techniques. With this wealth of material at hand, and the renewed popular interest in building with wood, the book grew naturally.

Although we have called it *The Complete Log House Book*, we realize that it does not include the valid opinions and procedures of people in this field whom we have not yet met or heard from. The craft of log building has become so eclectic that no single book could possibly cover every aspect in detail, though we have tried to give as complete a picture as possible. We would be happy to hear from anyone who would like to write to us about their experiences in log building.

We do not attempt to "sell" any particular style of log building here. We have tried to explain as objectively as possible the drawbacks as well as the obvious strong points of the various building methods. We have also tried to present you with a balanced overview, including as many options as possible, so you can choose the best kind of house for your own purposes.

Many of you who read our book might never actually build a log house. But we hope that you will have some enjoyable hours reading and looking at it, and that you will get a keener understanding of the energy and talent that goes into making these houses which are so much a part of our heritage.

Richard Skinulis

CHAPTER 1   looking back

A graphic illustration of early living conditions. Crude shelters were thrown up while the work of clearing the land and building a proper dwelling was done.

The tradition of building with logs goes back thousands of years. In his book, *De architectura,* written in the first century A.D., the Roman engineer and architect Vitruvius describes a method of building with logs which was used by the Colchi people around 30 B.C. The Colchi, who lived by the shores of the Black Sea, constructed the logs criss-cross fashion in a square, laying one log across the ends of the two logs below it, but not fitting them together at the corners. The spaces between them were filled with wood chips and mud. The logs were shortened as they reached the top of the structure to form a pyramid-shaped roof which was covered with leaves and mud.

For the first European settlers who came to North America, to New England in the United States and New France in Canada, their arrival at the docks in the New World must have seemed like landing on a strange new planet. While tramping down a gang plank after a gruelling three-month voyage in the hold of a crowded ship, the new immigrant's first thoughts were no doubt of a practical nature — how and where to get food and shelter. For the latter, a plot of land had to be cleared from the huge stands of virgin timber they saw all around them, and a rough shelter quickly put up to house the family through that first hard winter. Some were fortunate enough to get help and guidance from the

Indians, some managed to survive the first winter in makeshift dwellings of tree branches and bark, and some didn't survive at all. As soon as possible, the settlers set about building better houses in the way they were used to in their home country, rather than building log cabins as you might expect.

In *The Log Cabin Myth,* Harold Shurtleff shows that the English colonists of the seventeenth century were apparently unfamiliar with horizontal log-building techniques. They brought with them the frame and half-timber style of building germane to their homeland. For the first hundred years or so they were satisfied with this style in which hewn vertical timbers are erected and the spaces in between filled with bricks or stone (nogging) and plastered over, or covered over with whip-sawn (hand-sawn) boards. It was likewise with the early French in Canada and their *colombage* (half-timber) style, in which the spaces in between the vertical timbers were filled with fitted stone (*colombage pierrotté*) or horizontal, vertical or angled filler logs. The use of horizontal filler logs is known as the piece-on-piece method (from the French *pièce-à-pièce,* meaning bit by bit), a style of construction we discuss in Chapter 4. This style of building was later taken by the French to Western Canada, where it became known as Red River (or Manitoba frame) construction.

Therefore, contrary to popular opinion, the log cabin was not really the favored kind of dwelling of the early settlers. Up until the time of the American Revolution the few log structures were almost exact duplications of various Old World architectural styles. But after 1776, especially in Pennsylvania where many ethnic groups came together, European horizontal log

building techniques and English details such as window and door styles and proportions (those of a 15-x 16-foot cottage, possibly the space it took to house two yoke of oxen) were combined in log building. These influences produced the first distinctive North American log structure, a symbol of colonial independence and westward expansion.

The French colombage *style; in this case both vertical and angled logs were used as filler. Fortress of Louisbourg, Nova Scotia.*

A beautifully recreated French style pièce-en-pièce building built on a dry (mortarless) foundation. The techniques of the piece-on-piece method are discussed in Chapter 4. Fortress of Louisbourg, Nova Scotia.

A very secure-looking blockhouse located at Fort Ingall on Lake Temiscouata, Quebec, is a fine example of the neat, competent, military style. Notice the skillfully done keyed lap corners and well-hewn logs. In this instance, the logs were hewn to make the chinks between the logs smaller, rendering the building bullet-proof.

The first log structures in North America appear to have been not houses at all, but blockhouses built for military purposes. The logs in these buildings were generally hewn flat and squared off at the ends, the hewing and cutting to length often being done in the old country, and the logs shipped across to the colonies for quick and easy assembly. These buildings were done in that neat, competent military style that is somehow both admirable and uninspiring at the same time. This style of building was only used occasionally by early colonists — one of the first settlements in the United States was Fort St. George (now Phippsburg) at the mouth of the Kennebec River in Maine. It was built by the Virginia Company in 1607, and the buildings were made of horizontal logs slotted into vertical posts in the French fashion.

There are other examples of early log building in North American history, but historians generally agree that it was the Swedes who introduced to the New World the practice of building log houses. Horizontal log-building methods have had a long tradition in Scandinavia, Switzerland, Russia and Germany. The classic Scandinavian style is characterized by the round, tight-fitting logs with their distinctive protruding ends and saddle-notched corners (see Long Log section in Chapter 4). The Swedes began settling in Delaware around 1638, and the Germans arrived in Pennsylvania about 1710. In Pennsylvania, the Swedes, Germans, English and Scotch combined to produce the distinctive style known as

"Pennsylvania Dutch" (or more accurately *Deutsch*, meaning German). Therefore these particular styles of construction were obviously present in North America quite early, and one might think that the English settlers would have jumped at the chance to adopt these new methods, but they didn't.

Hence, log building existed only in small pockets on this continent until the Scotch-Irish started arriving around 1720. These were the Presbyterian Scottish tenant farmers who had earlier settled in Ulster on the land of the expelled Catholics. Some of

Square lap on round logs. Good enough for a hurried shelter or a barn. Note the mud and straw chinking. Black Creek Pioneer Village, Ontario.

As far as we know these notches are unique to this one particular building. Small wonder.

This corner is basically of the square lap type but note that three rows down from the top of the page the corners of one round of logs are dovetailed. This was probably done in the hope of keeping the building from bulging outward and buckling. The presence of these locking corners indicates that movement in square lap-jointed corners was a common, and in this case foreseen, problem.

Simple square lap. This type of corner is easy to cut but has two possible disadvantages. Water can easily run into the flat surface of the joint and will stay there causing decay. Movement caused by changes in heat and humidity can cause some logs to gradually work their way out of position.

Dovetail or self-draining dovetail. This type of joint does an excellent job of shedding water before it can run in between the faces of the joint. We have seen several buildings over a hundred years old in which the wood of the joint faces was as white as the day it was cut. The dovetail shape also stops any movement of the logs.

Saddle notch. The top side of each log is left round and the bottom of the log above is cut out to fit on over it. In this way the round sloping shape of each log top will prevent water from entering the joint. This method also locks the logs securely in place. For these reasons this is currently the most common method of cornering a round log building.

Compound dovetail. This joint has extra angles which the simple dovetail does not have. Although more interesting and complicated looking, it has no structural advantage.

Pennsylvania corners. A good system both for shedding water and for locking the logs in place. They are less common than the dovetail, probably due in part to the difficulty of cutting them. The top three notches are dovetails, probably an addition at a later date. The missing logs went down with the roof when it collapsed.

"Pig barn" corners. Wood is cut from both the top and the bottom of each log and water can easily rest in the joint. Two other corners of this same building were badly deteriorated. These should not be confused with saddle notches, although they look similar at first glance.

these settlers had emigrated to America when their leases expired. When they arrived in their new homeland, they readily embraced log construction as a cheap and easy method of building, and took it with them as they spread out to settle the American South and West. They seemed especially fond of the hewn logs and squared off corners made by the Germans, master craftsmen whose expertise in carpentry and fine joinery naturally included log work.

The Germans are also considered mainly responsible for the development of the Pennsylvania key notch (see photograph on page 15). Other common forms of notches (sometimes called *keying*) are shown on pages 14 and 15, and include the simple lap and keyed lap notches, and round saddle notches popularized by the Swedes. We have heard the saddle notch referred to, rather contemptuously, as "pig barn construction," a misnomer that confuses the well-done saddle notch with a less durable notch that cuts into both the bottom and the top of the log (see photograph on page 15).

It has been impossible to find out exactly who started using dovetail corners on log buildings, but our guess is that it was probably an enterprising English or German cabinetmaker-turned-builder who was familiar with this method of joining two pieces of wood, and applied it to log building. Two areas where full dovetail corners abound are the Ozark Mountains in the United States and Renfrew County, Ontario, in Canada.

One important result of the American Revolution was the migration northward to Canada of the United Empire Loyalists, those whose allegiance remained with the British. They brought with them the log-building methods of the Thirteen Colonies,

If the walls were stone instead of log, this rare two-storey house would have been perfectly at home in any upper-class neighborhood in Georgian England.

and these, coupled with the methods the French were already using, gave rise to a Canadian log-building tradition. In Canada, the settler's first home was known as a "shanty." This term probably derives from the French phrase used to describe the building where the lumberjacks were fed and housed, *une cambuse de chantier. Cambuse* means "a provision room" and *chantier* means "a lumber-yard." These words were Anglicized to make camboose shanty, and lumberjacks came to be known as shantymen.

The American counterpart of the Canadian shanty was the "log cabin."

The early settlers brought their architectural predispositions with them from their home countries. The family who settled this tract of land in Old Killaloe, Ontario, was obviously from the British Isles as this house is Georgian in every respect.

A typical camboose shanty, a temporary home in the bush near Lake Travers for fifty or sixty lumberjacks. The cook muses in the doorway, smoking his pipe.

The fire pit in a camboose shanty, the only source of heat and light. Below the four-foot square hole in the roof was an 8- x 10-foot area of bare ground enclosed with rocks and then filled with sand. A fire was lit on top of the sand and kept roaring day and night. Cooking pots were placed on or in front of the rocks and bread baked in the hot sand. Periodically the sand would "burn out" and refuse to heat up and have to be replaced.

Shantymen being served dinner inside a camboose shanty.

Both terms convey the feeling of a small rough-and-ready structure, built by people with much to do and little time and few materials to do it with. It is interesting to note that the dictionary defines the word "cabin," as a noun, as meaning "a small, crude dwelling," and, as a verb, as "to confine in a small place or cramp." So, it's no wonder that modern log builders cringe when their works are referred to as cabins by the uninformed.

A log cabin was usually a small, stacked-together round log building, with very small windows or none at all, and greased paper or even pickle jars (see photograph on page 19) used in window openings instead of glass. Sometimes there was just an open space that was covered up at night to keep the bugs and cold out, and a hide or piece of cloth for a door and a hole in the roof for the smoke to escape. The great advantage of a log cabin was that it reportedly took just two axemen only two days to put up a small, rough, eight-log (eight-foot high) shelter.

The term "log house" denotes a building made of large, well-fashioned logs, properly cornered, with the spaces in between the logs chinked with moss or branches, and well plastered with clay.

An early railroad worker's cabin built with Scandinavian-style round logs and saddle notch corners. The log gable ends support purlins and very small pole rafters.

A log cabin in disguise. Only the corners protruding from the plaster walls indicate what this house in Veregin, Saskatchewan, is really made of. A beautiful thatching job, it shows an Eastern European, perhaps Ukrainian, influence.

The windows should be made of glass; there are chimneys, a shingled roof, perhaps a small basement or root cellar, and probably more than one door. It would involve a high degree of workmanship, certainly much higher than that needed to build a log cabin. A log house would be higher than a cabin as well, perhaps 10 or 12 logs high, the extra logs forming what is known as a "knee-wall" above the second floor to provide head room for a loft; sometimes a log house would be two full stories high.

Log cabins were often built with the intention of being abandoned, or being used later as a shed or barn, or even as a summer kitchen attached to a new (permanent) house. There is historical evidence that cabins were sometimes burned down so a family could retrieve the precious nails from the ashes, when they moved on to their next homestead.

Every part of the log house has gone through stages of development. The roof, for instance, went from being simply layers of pine boughs to the "scooped roof," (see photograph on page 21), and then to crudely split cedar shakes. These early wooden shingles had no taper and gave the roof a bristly appearance. Because of the scarcity of nails during the early period of settlement, the rows of shingles were often held down with a network of heavy poles. The use of tapered cedar shakes, interlocking tin shingles and even factory-made roofing paper became widespread. At first, the roof structure itself was often made by building the front wall higher than the back and laying wooden scoops to drain the water. Alternatively, a simple crutch roof, made by placing forked poles at each end and securely lashing a ridge pole into the forks, created a crude kind of

Log huts and wooden markers over graves in a Jewish cemetery, Lipton Colony, Saskatchewan, 1906.

peaked roof with gable ends. This naturally progressed to the pole-rafter or post-and-purlin systems we discuss later in Chapter 2.

Floors, too, went from an utterly primitive to a more sophisticated form during the 150 years that was the heyday of log building. At first, a busy pioneer might just have a dirt floor, tamped down and swept daily. A wooden floor would have necessitated slabbing, taking straight-grained pine and splitting off slabs with a wedge,

Pickle jars were used instead of glass as windows in this simply-built log cabin. It has a purlin roof covered with sod and a lucky horseshoe on a peg.

A busy family working in their stump-littered front yard. The trees that were felled to clear the site would be used to build the cabin— a case of taking what you need from your surroundings. There probably wasn't a nail used in the entire structure. Even the chimney is made of logs, a style that is sometimes referred to as a "slave cabin" chimney.

and then hewing them with a broad axe. Later, boards from a saw mill were used.

The fireplace was the only means of cooking and heating. Cabin chimneys were poorly designed, and uncontrolled drafts from the fireplaces allowed great amounts of heat to go up and out with the smoke. These chimneys were made of small logs and clay, and are referred to as slave cabin chimneys. Log houses, on the other hand, would have had a brick or stone chimney. The invention and mass production of the cast-iron stove in the mid-nineteenth century, as well as the use of the lucifer match, made starting a fire

A Belgian immigrant in his newly-built log cabin near Millarville, Alberta.

This intriguing octagonal log structure is the Indian council house at Fort Albany, near James Bay.

and draft control much easier, so that the inefficient all-night fires became unnecessary. The cast-iron stove also allowed the overall size of the house to be expanded since it could now be heated in two separate areas and a single-storey summer kitchen also became possible. Since metal stove pipes kept more of the heat inside the house, they changed the shape of houses. No longer did people need to build big chimneys going up the outside end of the house — smaller chimneys on the roof were all that was needed.

One popular log cabin myth is that the availability of sawn lumber from the proliferation of saw mills caused the decline of log building. But we have seen too many log structures built with great numbers of mill-sawn boards to accept this theory. If well-chinked, the early log houses were warmer than the frame dwellings, mainly because at that time fiberglass insulation hadn't been invented.

The simple roof of this cabin was made by raising the front wall higher than the back and then using "scoops" to drain off the rain water. Scoops are logs (usually cedar or basswood) split in two, hollowed out and laid down like Spanish tiles.

Numerous log out-buildings on a farm carved out of the forest.

This woman who is waiting to get out of town is standing between a crudely built cabin and a nicely done house. The planks on the railroad tracks probably made them the only dry walkway in town.

A good example of a simple but solid log house. Notice the large, well-hewn logs, the neatly mortared chinks, well-notched dovetail corners and the large, glass windows. The two small chimneys on top indicate that this house was heated with cast-iron wood stoves.

A 1-1/2 storey house was often taxed as a single storey dwelling, which accounts for its popularity. In some areas, a house without front steps was considered unfinished and not taxed at all.

In pioneer communities across North America, the building of a log house was a focal point of social activity. Logs were an inexpensive and readily available building material for settlers all across the continent. Groups of neighbors got together whenever there was a new house or barn to be raised, so that a community really built its own buildings together. You are probably familiar with the stories of these bees — of how people from miles around would come streaming into a farm in the morning, the women cooking up immense pots of hearty fare, and the men forming themselves into different work parties. A foreman would be elected to supervise the work of the small army of workers, hewers and cornermen. In the case of a building that was not the round log (Scandinavian) type, the hewers would have the peeled logs brought to them, and then square them off on two sides. The cornermen were the most skilled axemen, and usually did all their work up on the wall so that they could keep rolling the logs into place, checking the progress of the notches. Everyone worked at a furious pace, and by the end of the day, the walls and roof rafters were all in place. After the house was up, and the sun going down, the young men would then race up to the top of the roof. The first one reaching the top had the honor of swinging an empty bottle three times around his head and throwing

A log smokehouse in the Champlain Trail Museum in Pembroke, Ontario.

Cobalt, Ontario. In the old days, when frontier towns seemed to spring up overnight, log buildings were often a quick and inexpensive way to get a business housed.

it into the surrounding fields. If it landed unbroken, it was considered an auspicious sign for the new house.

With their stomachs full of food, their ears still ringing with the wail of the fiddle, and their heads spinning from the home-made "licker," the pioneers rode their buckboards home to a log house that was probably very much like the one they had just helped to put up.

As more and more log buildings were put up, people naturally got better and better at the craft of building with logs. By the end of the nineteenth century, everything from tool sheds to castles were being built out of logs. But by the time of the Great Depression, the state of log building had declined.

There were, however, a few last ambitious stabs at building great log structures before the temporary fall from grace, and one of these was Le Chateau Montebello, which is one of the largest and most spectacular log buildings ever built.

Lucerne-in-Quebec Community Assoc.
Montebello, Que.
Photograph ..No.. 79.
Date Taken ..July 2nd
Title.. Log Lodge Seen from E

Le Chateau Montebello, situated on the Quebec side of the Ottawa river, is one of the largest log buildings in the world.

Interior of the main dining room showing some of the 3,500 men who worked on the Chateau.

The men on top are using hand augers to drill holes in the top logs so that they can be pegged into the logs below. Altogether over 10,000 western red cedar logs were used to build Le Chateau Montebello.

The first log was set in place on April 7, 1930, and all the log work was completed two months later.

A log church, still in active use, near Fort St. John in northern British Columbia.

Montebello is a huge, six-winged log hotel on the Ottawa River, 40 miles southeast of Ottawa. Originally a private club, the Seigneury Club, Montebello is now a Canadian Pacific hotel. It was big news in 1930 when it was built. Its mammoth size, the vast army of workmen orchestrated during its fantastically speedy erection, and the fact that it was made of logs, attracted huge crowds every weekend during its construction. The Chateau and adjacent buildings used a total of 10,000 western red cedar logs. The first log was set in place on April 7, 1930 — and all the

Russian Orthodox church on the prairies around the turn of the century.

log work was completed by June 7. This is an incredible feat when you consider the number of logs used, the precise nature of the scribing process and the fact that each log would have had to be moved at least half a dozen times before it finally rested in the wall. The cutting was done on an assembly-line basis. Most of the crew were Quebeckers, but many were Scandinavian craftsmen, skilled in the technique of scribing and V-grooving. At the height of construction, over 3,500 men had to be fed.

The quantities of material used for Montebello stagger the imagination: half a million hand-split cedar shakes, fifty-three miles of plumbing and heating materials, forty miles of electrical wiring, and 7,600 sprinkler heads carefully installed in prearranged patterns to accommodate the ceiling panels. Altogether, 1,400 doors and 535 windows, and 103 miles of wooden molding were needed!

On July 7, just four months after the excavation was begun, the Chateau was open for business. It has been standing for almost fifty years now, and will likely be around for many generations to come — a testament to log building and log builders.

In the 1930s and 40s, the log house had begun to fade in popularity. Their owners were covering up these overgrown structures with siding as if in shame. People started to identify them with penury or as being fit only as cottages and hunting lodges.

By the 1950s, many log houses were considered so valueless that they were burned down to reduce their owners' taxes. The old skills began dying out with the generation that they had served so well. Urban technology, geared to the needs of the mass market, reduced handcraft skills to an almost inaccessible luxury. Our future, it seemed, would be lived out in houses built as uniform products, an unfortunate reflection of our changing way of life. It wasn't until the late 1960s that the log renaissance began, and a new generation of builders rediscovered the old skills and the sheer joy of working with native wood.

design and planning

This beautifully proportioned house makes a successful blend of classic Georgian windows and doors, and the steep roofs and peaked dormers more common in French design.

Everyone would like a house that contains masterful joining work, functional doors and level floors, a house that sits high, dry and straight, ready to brave the elements for centuries to come. The achievement of fine craftsmanship should be pursued with dedication, but not to the extent that you become so obsessed with technical expertise that you ignore the importance of good design. In our travels and in our conversations with both amateur and professional builders, we have noticed that very few houses have been planned any further than the drawing up of rough floor layouts and, in our opinion, it often shows.

In the end, a house is not judged by a list of technical specifications, but rather by its action on human sensations. To the body it is warmth, coolness, comfort, relaxation and convenience; to the mind, peace and security. It provides light and stimulation for the eye, a balance of gaiety and dignity. These elusive sensations are sometimes difficult to appreciate while standing on the job site with your head full of numbers and your eyes full of sawdust. So make certain that you draw the house up on paper before beginning.

It has been said that beauty is only a matter of millimeters. Of course this is most often said about people, but it can be applied very well to architecture. For instance, the mathematical proportions which make a human face beautiful can in some sense be applied to houses.

The classic rectangular log (or frame) house is probably the most simple and basic example to draw from in this analogy. If you look at the photo on page 31, you may see a vague approximation of the human face. The roof can be seen as the hair and eyebrow line, the windows as eyes, and the entrance as the nose and mouth area.

The windows (the "eyes") are probably the most important area. Remember that the cartoonist makes great use of the eyes to denote expression in his characters. Small eyes close together are used to show confusion, drunkenness, or a myopic state. Eyes high in the face show surprise; low on the face, they show sadness; and with a heavy square accent over them, they look aggressive and intimidating.

The way you perceive the appearance of a house is governed by some very strong preconceived visual notions. The square, for example, is widely regarded as a rather boring and homely shape — a boring person is a "square," ugly houses are referred to as "little square boxes." The continuous flow of the circle on the other hand is exciting and powerful — think of the sun, cathedral domes, enchanted fairy circles — while the rectangle is as dignified as the classic Greek architecture which employed it so heavily. The relationship of shapes and proportions and their effect on human sensibility is a complicated study which has concerned some very great minds over the centuries. For this reason, time spent looking through books of classic architecture can be valuable to the person setting out to design his own house, although at first it may seem a bit irrelevant and pretentious.

We are not suggesting that you follow exactly any particular style of building, but we'd like to underline the importance of carefully considering your final result by looking at what good and bad buildings have been built in the past and learning from this.

A common pitfall to avoid is putting elements into the design of a building that are fine by themselves, but ones that will conflict when used together. Don't combine materials that are at odds with each other such as imitation wood paneling and a hewn beam ceiling, or bright aluminum storm doors on a log house.

There can also be a tendency to overdo a certain effect at the expense of the whole. Using too much wood is a mistake which many people can easily make because they have grown tired of seeing plain plaster walls and painted trim. People have lately become enamored with the appearance of natural wood. But a word of caution must be given against using too much wood and eliminating drywall altogether. Plaster and wood complement each other very well. In a log room with wooden doors, floors, ceilings and walls, the natural beauty becomes obscured and commonplace because there are no other materials offering a visual contrast. The early inhabitants of this country quickly discovered that living in a house of wood in a nation of trees can become rather oppressive. They loved paint. A lot of those pine antiques which people are patiently stripping to their "original" wood finish have actually been painted since day one, sometimes with the brightest colors available.

White or off-white ceilings and partition walls can greatly improve the feeling of spaciousness of a room, making it generally more cheerful, and helping to focus the eye on the natural beauty of the wood that is used to maximum effect.

Unless you are deliberately setting out to create dramatic contrasts in your design, you should keep an eye on balancing the appearance of your house. The concept of balance is considered so important in some types of design such as Georgian and Victorian that windows can appear in such unlikely places as closets! The sole purpose of this is to give the exterior of the building perfect continuity and balance. You may also find houses in which windows have been bricked up since the building was new, leaving only a stone sill, brick lintels and a joint line in the bricks where the window frame would normally have been. Obviously, some element of interior design had made it undesirable to have a window in this position, whereas from outside the window was needed to balance the appearance of the house. These examples may seem a bit extreme but they show the importance several well-developed schools of architecture place on a balanced design.

One example of extremely bad balance may be understood if you imagine moving one of the front windows of the house in the photo on the opposite page right over to within one foot of the corner, leaving the massive visual weight of the upper logs and roof supported by only a thin leg. Also imagine the effect of making one window much larger than the other, or of removing one altogether. This idea may seem obvious in the case of the house pictured in the photo; but with a large and complicated dwelling, the necessary balance

The gothic tone of the trim details on this home in Collingwood suggests that it was originally built for a man of the church.

becomes more easily thwarted by some need of the interior design.

Interior wood trim is another area in which tradition has placed great importance on balance. The term "return" figures frequently in trim detail. Certain elements have actually taken on that name, such as the plaster molding at the top of a wall, sometimes referred to as a "return" because it is an approximate reverse image of the baseboard and serves to return the effect begun by it. When the moldings which form the top rail of wainscoting or wall paneling reach a door or other stopping point, they will turn the corner and return into the wall, their overhang on the **end** being the same as their overhang on the **front** of the paneling. They are thereby returned rather than ending abruptly in a square end, flush with the end of the paneling.

Another common error of amateur house design is putting a doorway so close to an adjoining partition wall that there is no room for trim, thereby creating a lopsided and unpleasant effect.

THE DESIGN PROCESS

The only way to arrive at a reasonably accurate idea of what your house will look like is to draw it up, inside and out. Don't shy away from this extremely important job, hoping that it will all work out in the end or thinking that you can keep it all straight in your head. You don't need to have any special education or talent to do a good job — thoughtfulness and perseverance will suffice. And if you think that drawing will waste valuable time — erasing and moving little lines, ad nausea, — just give some thought to the time and expense involved in moving those lines once they have become huge timbers and

complicated frame details. Your house represents one of the biggest investments in time, money and emotion that you are ever likely to make. The amount of time and trouble you spend in planning it can never be too much.

Before beginning the actual planning you will obviously find it a great help to look at what others have done. We have compiled a bibliography at the end of this book which should provide some inspiration. When thinking over the various plans which might appeal to you it is important to keep in mind some factors other than the visual impression of a certain style. Consider natural light, heat efficiency, noise travel, convenience and simplicity — all in relation to your own

Although attractive for the most part, this house design is marred by the dormers which are too small for the main roof, and awkwardly placed as well. If you look closely at the far right-hand corners you will notice the absence of the usual interlocking corners. What appears to be a log building is actually a frame structure made from thick slabs of wood, complete with tree bark edges, nailed onto the exterior. Plaster has been put between them to imitate chinking.

specific needs. Go out and look at as many actual houses as possible, rather than getting all your ideas from books. In doing this you will get a realistic impression of how different designs and materials actually feel.

Doing a Rough Estimate

Before you can put anything down on paper, you will have to decide how big to make your house. Unfortunately this decision is most frequently controlled by how much you can afford rather than how much you need or want. Take the cost factors as best you can determine them and add a dash of pessimism for good measure.

The cost of building a house can be estimated in terms of so many dollars per square foot of floor area. This method may not be entirely accurate, but it's more accurate than you may think at first glance. Decide whether your house is to be basic, moderate or luxury in style. Factors to keep in mind while doing this are these: the number of windows and doors; the quality and extent of finishing details; extras such as saunas; the number of bathrooms, etc. Now call around to a few builders and real estate people in your area, and ask them what the square foot costs of houses of similar quality have been. People in this business are used to thinking in terms of cost per square foot and they will not find such a question unusual. Divide the amount of money available by the cost per square foot, and you will have the size of your house. For example if you have found that moderately-priced housing is costing $30 per square foot, and you have $30,000 to work with you can afford a completed one-storey house of 1000 square feet, or a two-storey house of 500 square feet per floor. Only the square footage of living area is counted. Don't count the basement area in this estimate unless it is to be the walkout type, in which case an allowance will have to be made. Walkout basements, completely finished, can come very near the cost of regular above-ground work.

The price you have estimated for your house will of course be based on a house with standard walls. Here we are concerned with log walls. Since each log house will be quite different in cost of materials and amount of time consumed in construction, there is no hard-and-fast rule that may be applied. However, our experience has been that a log wall generally costs the same (if not a bit more) than a regular wood-sided standard frame wall when costs of labor are included. Without the inclusion of labor costs they can be somewhat cheaper. If the house you are planning goes further than log walls (i.e., using logs for beam ceilings and floors), more price adjusting will be necessary.

Another rough estimating device which may be helpful is that in rough carpentry work such as framing and sheathing, the cost of the materials will be about two-thirds of the final cost, and the cost of labor one-third. For example, if you wanted to know the total cost of a roof, you would add up the value of all the parts, divide that by two and multiply by three. For finish and trim work, the ratio is closer to one part labor to one part materials. These same formulas may also be used to estimate the amount of time required to do a certain job. Take the figure for labor costs and divide it by the average hourly pay rate for that particular trade. This gives you the number of hours required. Figures obtained by these methods certainly cannot be guaranteed to be entirely accurate, but they can be a real help in the rough planning stages.

Another factor to consider in planning the size of your house is the minimum size requirements of the township that you live in. It may seem astonishing that any government body should be able to dictate how big you must build your own house, but they can.

In the case of our own projects involving reconstructed hewn log houses, we found that we could turn up with an end price per square foot which was the same or just slightly higher than the cost of comparable housing of standard wood construction. The money saved by using reclaimed doors, beams, flooring, etc., was quickly offset by the cost of the considerable amount of time required to re-work them, and fit them together. The amount of labor required to build a log house is much greater than that required by standard construction techniques.

Some people who specialize in the long log style of building tell us that the end price of their houses also cannot be expected to be below the price of standard housing.

We say this here in the hopes of dispelling any notions that by building a log house of used materials or trees from the bush, you may somehow bypass the normal laws of economics. This just isn't so, unless you are willing to count your time as having no value. Even then, the cost of nails, cement, excavating, roofing, windows, etc., will add up to a considerable amount. In short, don't start out to build a log house thinking that, through some miracle, you can finish it at a cost far below regular building.

We have had some people ask us to build them just the shell of a log house finished to the point where they could live in it while they themselves did the finishing work. They hoped in this way to be able to greatly stretch their money. We pointed out that by the time a log house is weather tight and equipped well enough for them to live in, it is virtually finished. The work

The slanted drip ledge at the base of the gable end sheathing boards causes rainwater to drop off away from the wall of the house. Side casing around the edge of the window trim guarantees a good seal between the trim and the wall of the house, preventing the entry of wind, rain and insects. The short return of the fascia board and eavestroughs (the eave line) on the face of the gable end increases the protection of the corner joints. Also the continuance of the eave line on the gable end visually ties the lines of the house together. The fluted molding which is nailed to the fascia board and supports the shingle edges not only looks attractive, but its support of the shingles enables them to overhang the fascia boards farther and more completely protect them from the weather.

Handsome proportion and careful detailing in this house reflect the touch of an architect who knows his subject and a builder who takes pride in his skill. Together with the owner, they have created a well-balanced and inviting residence in the fine style of a bygone century.

The siding boards are carefully spaced so that the battens which cover the cracks between them occur in exactly the same place under each window. The short eavestroughs between the dormers serve more to improve the visual continuity of the eave line than any practical purpose. The metal flashing in the valley between the dormers and the main roof increases in width toward the bottom to accommodate the larger amount of ice and snow which will collect there and may force its way under the shingles. The shingles at the eaves are also doubled to prevent ice from backing up under them.

The protruding course of bricks at the base of the chimney creates a drip ledge for any water running down the upper face of the chimney, thereby decreasing the amount of water which must be repelled by the chimney base flashing.

The subtle curve of the porch trim quietly adds its contribution to the overall appearance without drawing attention to itself.

that can be done after the point of moving in amounts to a fairly small percentage of the total cost of the house.

Setting out to build a house with plans much larger than your resources can turn a pleasant and enlightening process into a chore and a burden, at best described as a good lesson.

Once your house has taken a fairly definite shape you may be able to arrive at a more exact cost by making up a detailed list of costs of all materials, labor, mechanical contracts, etc. This is a lengthy and difficult project in which we have found that the tendency is to err on the side of underestimating. Things are easily overlooked when making the list, but rarely are things added which become unnecessary later. Similar acts of omission coupled with mistakes due to optimism tend to make the final estimated price smaller, rather than larger, than is realistic. *Note:* When estimating lumber needed, always add ten percent to account for waste.

Contracting

When you are gathering price estimates for work that someone else is doing for you, always get at least two, if not three, estimates on the same job. We have encountered situations in which the price of estimates to do the same piece of work varied as much as fifty percent. If, for example, that fifty percent difference represents a saving of $500, and the gathering of extra estimates takes eight hours of your time, that works out to $62.50 per hour. We consider that time well spent.

We don't suggest that you should always take the lowest bid. You must assess whether all the people who have

A functional arrangement of the work center in a large kitchen.

bid on the job are capable of doing the work with the same attention to quality and whether they are likely to show up on time and do the work as promised. Make sure that each person bidding has the exact same information regarding what is required so that the bids will be comparable.

Always write and have signed a complete and detailed list of exactly what is to be done, what materials will be used, when it will be done and how much it will cost. Don't be shy to be businesslike in this matter. Honest contractors will appreciate such a clear and specific agreement to dispel any future disputes over exactly what was or was not said. If the contractor turns out to be less than

honest, this paper will be your only legal control over him. It could save you a lot of trouble — and cash.

Purchasing Materials

Take your time when shopping for materials. Lumber sales people are accustomed to calls from customers fishing for good prices and you shouldn't hesitate to call several to get the best price. Once again, make sure that you are always talking about the same quality of material with each supplier. With lumber it

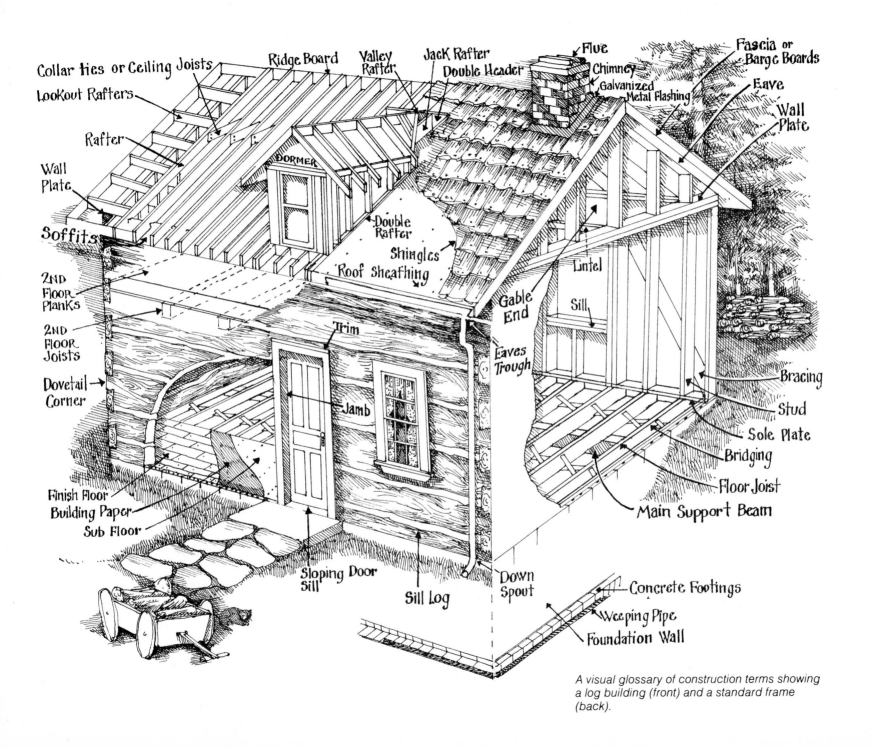

Collar ties or Ceiling Joists

Lookout Rafters

Rafter

Wall Plate

Soffits

2ND FLOOR PLANKS

2ND FLOOR JOISTS

Dovetail Corner

Finish Floor
Building Paper
Sub Floor

Ridge Board

Valley Rafter

Jack Rafter

Double Header

DORMER

Double Rafter

Shingles

Roof Sheathing

Trim

Jamb

Sloping Door Sill

Sill Log

Flue

Chimney

Galvanized Metal Flashing

Fascia or Barge Boards

Eave

Wall Plate

Lintel

Gable End

Sill

Eaves Trough

Bracing

Stud

Sole Plate

Bridging

Floor Joist

Main Support Beam

Down Spout

Concrete Footings

Weeping Pipe

Foundation Wall

A visual glossary of construction terms showing a log building (front) and a standard frame (back).

is always best to go out and look at what you are buying, rather than ordering by phone, since the quality can vary widely. All lumber is graded and marked with a number and a class, but some suppliers are more lax than others in applying grading rules.

DRAWING UP YOUR PLANS

Now that you have begun to grasp the magnitude of the project, you can begin drawing it up. It is best to begin with small rough sketches called "thumbnails." These can be done freehand or on graph paper using each square to represent one foot of floor space. Minimum size guidelines for various types of rooms are shown in a chart in the appendix.

Begin with a diagram of the lot layout. Mark on it the angle and path of the winter and summer sun, the direction of the winter wind, the view, drive and parking areas, the location of the septic tile bed and any other factors which may be relevant to your particular building site.

Some additional questions to keep in mind:

1. Will the winter sun come into your daytime rooms to warm them or into your bedrooms, where perhaps you don't want it except in early morning?
2. Will the morning sun come into your kitchen to make it cheerful or will the afternoon sun come in making it a bit hotter than you will like?
3. Will the full blast of winter wind hit a whole wall of windows and doors, or will it hit a solid wall?
4. Snow drifts will pile up on the leeward side of the house, or any abrupt nearby hills. Will this happen right in front of your entrance way?

5. Does your bedroom look out onto the approach to your house so that visitors driving up early Sunday morning can be seen without your having to get dressed to run across the house to a window?
6. Is the kitchen and basement entrance close and accessible enough to where you park to facilitate bringing in supplies?

All these things will have different values depending on your priorities, the type of house you are building, and the location. Sometimes you'll have to trade one advantage off against another.

Do rough floor plans for all levels and parts of the house. There is no sense in finishing a perfectly detailed first floor plan, then finding out that you have to move the stairs because of a problem with the second floor or basement, thereby making it necessary to alter the plans for the other floors. While laying out the various rooms, mark in a number which will indicate to you the relative noise level of each room. It is best to avoid putting the children's play area right over your quiet study. The acoustics of a house are a very subtle but very important point, often overlooked until too late.

In a multi-level house you may find it an advantage to do your rough layouts on tracing paper. You can save time and improve accuracy by tracing the basic outline (stairs, chimney, etc.) of the first floor onto the basement and second floor plan. This method will enable you to see the house more clearly in its three-dimensional aspect. It will also help prevent easy mistakes in the transferring of dimensions from one floor to the next. Keep moving rooms around, changing sizes and window or door locations, until you have what you want where you want.

Watch out for rooms that are too long and narrow to be of good use, or hallways and access doors that are too small to move furniture through. Try to eliminate dead spaces and traffic circulation problems. As your rough plans come near to completion, it will help to take a mental tour of the inside and outside of the house. Close your eyes and imagine yourself going through the house on your various missions of pleasure and work — carrying in groceries, reading beside a window, cooking in the kitchen, having a party, carrying the laundry around or groping for light switches in the dark. With a little practice, you should be able to take a mental tour of the whole house, and see in your mind's eye every part of every room. This will help to catch details that you have missed.

As the rough floor layouts take shape, you will have to be working coincidingly on the exterior plan, making sure that the roof line, window placement, etc., are both possible and desirable. The interior and exterior designs are of course inseparable and must always be developed together.

For those of you who are reconstructing an old house, you will be further limited by the placement and size of the original openings. Reconstructors should keep an eye out for opportunities to correct inherent faults in the building they are working with. A rotten wall may be the one chosen to turn toward an adjoining section of the new house, or an unwanted door cutout may become the wall opening for the back of the fireplace. The method for getting rid of cutouts in the log walls is shown in the illustration on page 102. Plugging holes this way should only be done as a last resort if the opening cannot be dealt with in the arrangement of the layout because it is a time-consuming process and it is difficult to end up with a "good-as-new" result.

Here is a checklist to run through during both the rough and final planning stages:

1. Do the doors swing into an unusable space or are they going to ruin a planned seating arrangement or interfere with passage of traffic?
2. In a one-and-a-half storey design, make sure that the doors you have planned will work without hitting the slope of the roof and that the stairs don't end at a sloping ceiling where you won't have room to stand.
3. When planning the floor openings for the stairs, remember to account for the thickness of the floor (including joists) when calculating head clearance or the length of the openings. Also make sure that the opening is wide enough to allow for hand rails, including knuckle clearance, and that you accounted for stair railings when calculating the width of the hallways.
4. Are the doors far enough away from the corners and intersecting walls so that there will be adequate space for the style of trim which you are planning?
5. Are your window sizes so large that they will be too close to the second floor beams to allow for the width of the trim?

Heating Design

In planning for the heat system, there are a few things you should take into account on the drawings. In a forced air heat system there is one large main duct or "plenum" which comes out of the furnace and runs across the ceiling at right angles to and underneath the ceiling joists. This large plenum feeds smaller pipes which run up from it into the space between the joists, and from there across the house to the floor vents or to pipes which will take the hot air to the second floor. Because the main plenum runs underneath the basement ceiling joists, it can interfere with head clearance, doorways, main beams, etc. The size of the plenum will vary with regard to the capacity of the furnace. If the basement is to have finished walls, add to this the thickness of the framing and sheathing which will enclose it.

The riser pipes which take heat to the second floor can also be a problem in log construction, as there are no exterior walls which they can be placed inside. We have found it necessary to run them up through interior partition walls or even inside the masonry of the fireplace. Each time a heating pipe is made to turn a corner, the volume of air delivered at the end is drastically reduced, almost by half, so it is wise to avoid having too many turns in any one pipe.

Hot air vents or hot water radiators are generally placed near exterior walls or under windows so that the full force of the heat can warm these potentially cooler areas, and the movement of the hot air will prevent a build-up of cold air pockets.

The large cold air return vent which feeds air back to the furnace should be placed well away from hot air inlets. It should also be kept away from seating areas to prevent the cold air from blowing by you on its way to the furnace. In a two-storey design with an open staircase, the cold air return vent should be placed at the bottom of the stairwell to the side of the stairs, to catch the cold air as it falls down the stairs. Cold air can be run through the spaces between the floor joists, eliminating the need for duct work. There is no need to draw all of the details

of the heat system onto your plans, but you must have a clear idea of where the major plenums are to run so that you can properly locate stairs and main beams and can determine the direction in which the floor joists should run.

The Mechanical Room

It is a good idea to group mechanical systems such as pumps, water heaters and the furnace in one room in a corner of the basement. Closing them off in this way will minimize the amount of motor noise traveling to the rest of the house. It will also make it possible to install a small thermostat-controlled electric heater in the room which will turn on automatically in the event of a furnace failure while you are away, protecting the equipment from freezing. People who plan to leave their house for extended periods in the winter should take extra care to install their plumbing so that all pipes can be easily and completely drained before leaving. This could prevent a frozen and burst pipe from badly damaging the house when it thaws in the morning. We can't begin to tell you what a house looks like after a frozen pipe on the second floor has burst, then thawed again, and the pump has been running full blast for two weeks while the owners have been away!

FINAL PLANS

Now that your rough plans are well under way, and you have a more concrete idea of what your house consists of, you should begin the finished plans. At this stage you should measure everything out exactly, using the scale of 1/4 inch per foot, showing wall thickness and using exact sizes

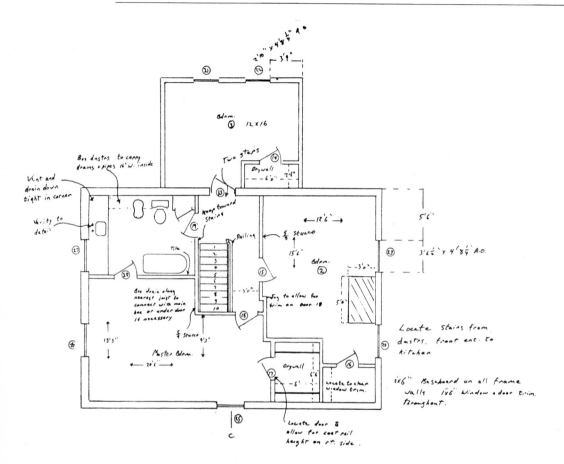

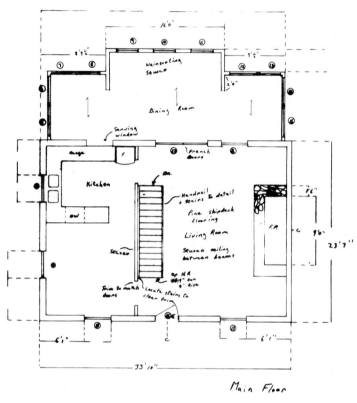

Main Floor

for windows, doors, etc. Draw on sheets of tracing paper large enough to leave a space on either side of the drawing for marking dimensions and notes. Tape the paper to a piece of plywood which has a straight edge on the right side. A T-square can then be run along this edge with the blade of the square extending to the opposite side of the paper which is on the board. Use this to mark horizontal lines. A large drawing triangle with a 90-degree corner is then placed on top of the

blade of the T-square and is used to mark vertical lines. Using this system rather than just a pencil and ruler will give you instant right angle corners and make it unnecessary to measure the length of any more than one of any series of parallel lines. You will find this a big time-saver. Tracing paper is used so that each floor outline can be traced from the previous one. Also, if you go over these lines in ink when plans are finalized, you can have blueprint copies made of them at very little

expense. This will give you copies to hand out to the mechanical trades when getting estimates, to the building department for the permit, and to friends who are helping so they will know what is going on. It also helps prevent the originals from perishing in chain saw oil and high winds!

Begin by doing the first floor plan. Just do the basic shapes, leaving the marking of dimensions and embellishments until later. Be as exact as possible with wall thicknesses, counter widths, staircases,

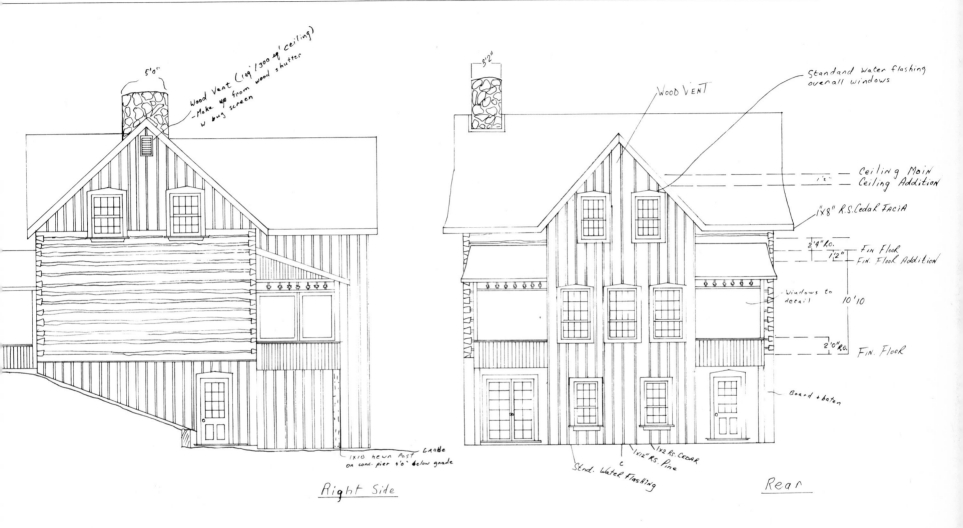

Right Side

Rear

etc. A few inches here or there can really alter the function of some spaces especially in closets and kitchens.

Now lay over this a fresh sheet of paper and do the plan for the basement. In log construction the basement should be at least ½ inch smaller than the main log work on all sides so the logs will overhang the foundation, allowing water to run off

rather than run inside. Mark in your main support columns and beam. These will be located and sized in relation to the spans allowable for the floor joists you are using. This size information is best found in the tables of the building code in effect in your area or in one of the standard frame construction books listed in the bibliography.

These are plans we did for the house which appears on pages 106 and 107.

Don't forget to mark in the footings for the fireplace. Make sure that the floor joists run in a direction that will best suit the layout of the heating pipes if you have forced air heat. Again, just do the bare bones of the shapes, leaving the detailing

Protruding casement window units add interest to a part of a board and batten addition which may have been too expansive and blank otherwise.

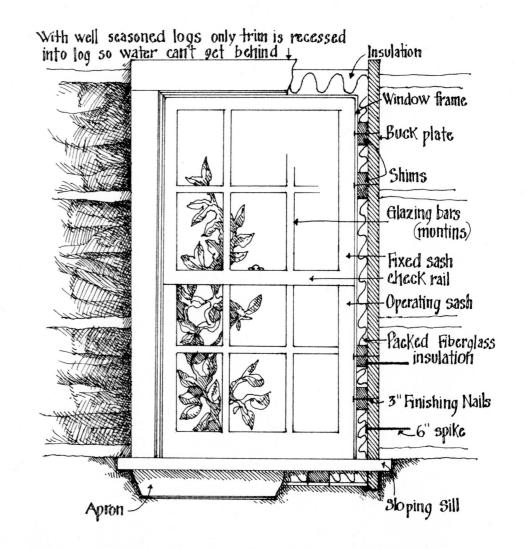

With well seasoned logs only trim is recessed into log so water can't get behind ↓

Insulation

Window frame

Buck plate

Shims

Glazing bars (montins)

Fixed sash check rail

Operating sash

Packed Fiberglass insulation

3" Finishing Nails

6" spike

Apron

Sloping Sill

Cut-away of double-hung window showing details.

until later. If the second floor doesn't work out you may have to alter all of the plans to agree with a new placement of the stairs or some other problem area.

Once the outline of the basement is marked in and suitable, take it off and do the second floor plan, if any. When that is done, go over the checklist and all the plans right back to the exterior lot plan to make sure that everything suits you.

Now with the first floor plan on the board, put on a clean sheet of paper and begin the exterior front. Your window placement and wall sizes can then be transferred directly by looking through the paper to the floor plan underneath. This is quick and will avoid mistakes in the transfer of measurements.

The front and one side of the building should be done on the same piece of paper or on separate sheets taped to the drawing board side by side. This is done so that once you have completed one face or "elevation" of the house, you may use the T-square to transfer the location of some points such as the roof apex, floor heights, gable end heights, and line of the eaves from the first finished drawing

WINDOWS AND DOORS

Your windows and doors are the light and life of your house. They are the focal point and backbone of your design, controlling the basic character more than any other feature. They are the eyes of the creation.

Windows

The classic log house window is the double-hung type, in which the sash slides up and down. These windows were always composed of small panes of glass divided by muntin or glazing bars. The small size of the panes was necessitated by primitive glass rolling techniques, window panes becoming larger as time went on; four or five panes wide before 1820 (when glass frequently had a blue oil slick appearance); three panes wide by 1835; two panes wide by 1870; one sheet by 1890 (from *Building with Wood* by John Rempel).

The double-hung system was probably not chosen so much for its weatherproof working, but rather because it was the staple of fine Georgian architecture which the British settlers had left behind in the old country. The elegant proportions of the Georgian window, always taller than wide, were considered by some to have reached perfect proportion when the height was twice the width, or a square over a square. Classic Georgian proportion can be seen in all its simplicity in the photo on page 16.

More than a thing of beauty, the double-hung window is a very practical design which will operate properly for a long time and adapts well to modern conveniences such as storm windows and screens. The bevelled edge of the check rail (see sketch on opposite page) causes

directly onto the one you do next. Once again, this is done to save time and improve accuracy.

To do the drawing of the back of the house you can sometimes trace the outline of the front to give the basic shape to begin with. The outlines of the sides are also reverse images of each other with some houses. To get the second side, just trace the outline of the first, then flip the paper over. The reversed outline will now show through the tracing paper.

When you have all the outlines of the drawings juggled into place so that they suit you, go back over them and mark in

A successful solution to the problem of achieving modern window size while still maintaining a "period" look.

the details. Don't do anything in ink until the very last.

Good plans can save a lot of time and costly errors in figuring the window and door sizes, lumber and material orders, location of lighting, etc. The end result of this sometimes painstaking work will be a house you can enjoy and be proud of.

the sash to move apart as the window is closed and the check rails meet, forcing the sash against the stop rails and thereby sealing out the wind. The only weather stripping which might possibly be necessary would be where the sash meets the sill.

The glazing bars are a feature of log house windows which are almost a necessity in our view. Large solid panes in a window can give it a very blank and stark appearance, especially from the outside. A lot of people are tempted to avoid small window panes because of the considerable extra work involved in cleaning and painting. If this is really a major point with you, it could be resolved by the use of large sheets of glass with glazing bar grills that snap into place and remove for cleaning. These are available from most modern window manufacturers to go with your units. If you are using thermal glass windows to eliminate the need for storm windows, you will find these clip-on grills indispensible, as making thermal glass in a series of small panes is a very difficult and costly process.

Nearly all modern double-hung windows are made using thermal glass or double glazing systems which eliminate the need for the storms. Some types can even allow both the upper and lower sash to be rotated inwards so they can be cleaned from the inside. These modern systems can prevent you from ruining a perfectly good weekend every year defying the laws of gravity with a can of window cleaner or a storm sash in your hand.

The purist who finds that the appearance of these modern hardware systems spoils the perfection of detail as the eye moves around the house may well decide to go all the way with the old style. In this case the best system we have found for

putting on storm windows is to use an aluminum storm whose metal is factory anodized to a color close to the final color of the window unit. These storms should be put in place before the exterior trim is put on. They can now be sized and fashioned in such as way that when the trim is applied it will cover almost all the aluminum frame at the edge of the unit.

The storm, when applied in this way, will all but disappear. If even this small inroad to modernity is too much for you, you are left with wooden storms. When you put these on, hang them from special hinges which are available for this purpose so they can be swung open to admit fresh air when necessary. Watch out for those sliding screen units, which go in under the open sash and expand until they meet the sides of the frame. Bugs can still enter freely because the check rail is now parted, so they can enter between the two sashes.

OTHER WINDOW STYLES

The casement window (see photograph on page 42) operates by swinging either in or out on hinges. These windows can be very pretty and give a pleasant feeling to the house, but some problems are inherent. If they are made to swing in, they interfere with room space. If they swing out, they stand a good chance of being ripped off by a sudden wind. Also, they are impossible to get at when a screen or storm is in place and must then be operated by an inside-mounted crank assembly. Note that a center-fixed rail is necessary between the sash so that they can be pulled tight and sealed against the rail. Because of these drawbacks the casement window has been most popular

This fine bit of craftsmanship, a refugee from a demolished church, retains its original large two-way spring hinges to provide easy "hands-off" access to the kitchen it serves.

in Mediterranean climates, although it can now be satisfactorily used in colder climes with the advent of modern interior hand cranks and thermal glass.

The horizontal sliding window is, in our opinion, an atrocity in all but the most modern style of round log buildings. The main advantage of this type of window is that it is cheap in relation to other styles. Its long and low appearance can have no other effect than to make the building look modern. This style of window is not available with glazing bars, and would look incongruous if they were added.

If the horizontal sliding window is called

DOORS

The straight-lined elegance of these doors with their small, discrete brass knobs is not traditional log house fare, but their suitability cannot be denied.

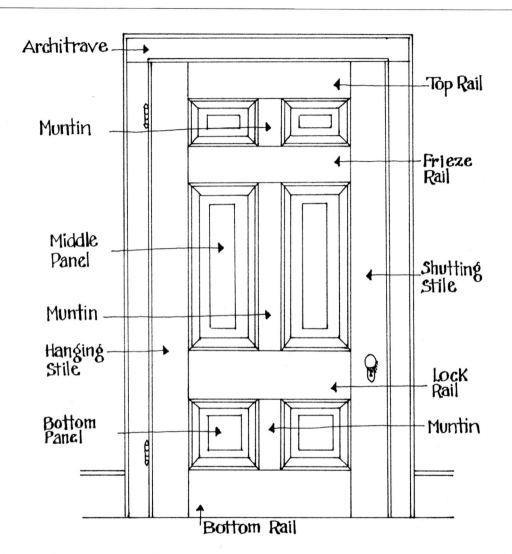

for in the design which you wish to have, be sure to avoid the common type in which sashless sheets of glass slide in grooves cut in the frame. They stick and jam, the knobs get pulled off and the little levers which are supposed to push them together to seal them are no more than advanced wishful thinking. Also, when ice forms in the track it will freeze your window in whichever position you last left it. The amount of heat escaping through this fifth-rate setup will pay the difference for better units in short order. The better units have wooden sashes around the sheets of glass and these sashes slide in well-designed weather stripping units.

Doors

Doors are a fine place for the patient creator of beautiful woodwork to reach the fullest expression of the craft. Every person entering your house will unavoidably encounter the door. It also likely has some semi-magical role to fulfil in protecting the inhabitants against the boogeys of the outside world. Making the front door is a good rainy-day shop project, something to fiddle with as you are dreaming up the

Four-panel exterior door with stained glass transom.

This heavy pine plank door gives a feeling of solid security, but unfortunately this type of door has a tendency to warp.

Four-panel door with raised panel trim.

house and longing to actually get at building it.

Through these pages you will find pictures of several classic as well as original door designs. Unless you are aiming for a certain classic style you are free to use any type of door that strikes your fancy. But bear in mind that a good solid wood exterior door should be of the panel type (see illustration on page 46) to avoid warping and twisting which is not only unattractive, but lets air in around the seals. Solid plank doors of tongue-

and-groove boards fastened together by other boards running crossways will serve best only for closet doors, if at all. No matter how dry the wood, the boards will often twist, shrink or expand enough to be noticed. This problem is accentuated in the case of an exterior door which must tolerate different temperatures and humidity on the inside and outside surfaces. If you are going to make some interior doors out of planks — it is both attractive and economical — you should do one thing differently than you might think. Instead of clamping the planks together as tightly as possible before gluing and screwing the horizontal braces

on, leave a space of about $1/8$ inch between each board and leave out the glue. This will allow each board to expand separately rather than all together as a unit, greatly reducing the overall movement of the wood.

If you like the sturdy look of a plank door for the exterior you can do as Lydia Vanderstaal has done in the photograph on page 154 and build a thin frame which is sheeted with tongue-and-groove on both the inside and the outside, separate from each other. Again leave a small space between each board. The size of the space will have to be determined by how dry the lumber is and whether it is

These double doors could use a coat of paint or varnish to halt their obvious deterioration. Although they look good where they are, they would have perhaps been better suited to interior use where the problem of sealing them against the weather would be eliminated.

This door was built for a log home in southern Ontario but its Greek columns and peaked cornice are clearly of the "Federal" style which was common on the East Coast of the United States. The original owner was likely a United Empire Loyalist, fleeing the American Revolution.

Entrance ways with windows all around, such as this one, were the mark of the house of a gentleman of means in pioneer days. The round top panels and elaborate cornices are rather rare gothic overtones.

expected to shrink or swell later.

The problems of expansion and contraction are partially avoided in panel doors as the panels can slide in grooves in the main frame and will allow much more movement without forcing the door out of shape.

RECYCLING OLD DOORS

Old doors from wrecked houses are our favorites. They were generally built with precision and quality materials, carefully planned and properly proportioned. When the paint is off and they are refinished, the old wood has a glow and color that cannot be matched. However, there are several things to watch for when trying to reuse doors.

An old door will usually be covered in several coats of paint. The paint could hide things which might make the door unusable when the paint is stripped off. Watch out for plywood panels in newer vintage doors. Plywood doesn't lend well to a natural finish. Take a good look around the area where the latch mechanism is mounted. See that it hasn't been replaced at one time or other and the old holes plugged and painted over. An old door which has been reversed in the past will have wooden plugs opposite the existing latch. Also look out for bad doggie scratches — many doors are ruined by dogs. Before making the opening that the door will fit into check that the door itself is square. They have often been planed in the past to stop them from jamming and can be really out of shape. If they are not straight and square make them that way before taking their final measure. If the present hinge cutouts are not exactly what you will be using again — they usually aren't — cut a narrow strip off the door to get rid of them altogether. Most kinds of stripping processes leave the wood wet and expanded for a while after. Any door should be in the house it is intended for, if possible, for a week or two to allow it to take on its usual moisture content, and hence, size. This will avoid some later refitting.

Try to pick out your fittings, doors, windows, hardware, etc., as much in advance as possible. It would be a sad thing if you found yourself in a tight corner with bad weather coming on or a move-in date fast approaching and you had to rush out to the local building supply store and use off-the-shelf fittings. Your beautiful log work should never have the subdivision look inflicted on it. Take time before the main part of construction to decide what you will need. Make up what is called a "schedule" of your window sizes, and one for your doors as well. Start compiling a list of the hardware that you will need. Old doors and fittings must be collected before the project begins so you will know what size to make the rough openings. If you enjoy the luxury of having a great deal of time, for instance a whole winter before a spring start, you're in luck. Go around to

antique auction sales and keep an eye out for those little baskets of junk that are frequently sold as a unit and can often contain beautiful old hinges, door knobs, latches, etc. Go to wrecking yards around your area and see what you can pick up. Keep in touch with the wreckers to find out when buildings come up for demolition. You will often find that the good stuff is snapped up before it even makes it to the yard. It is desirable to get most of the doors from the same house so you can maintain continuity throughout your plan.

Don't buy used pieces of trim unless you can be sure that you will have enough to complete the whole job. Making a new piece of trim to match an old one is a time-consuming process. Be cautious about buying old window units, as the time required to refinish and repair them can often make them a losing proposition.

For new doors and windows go down to your lumber supplier and ask for pamphlets from the manufacturers. These will tell you what fittings are available and in what sizes. This information is indispensable to the making of plans, as you will have to design for standard available sizes. One surprising thing that we have found is that we can often have windows and doors custom made by a small local shop just as cheaply (if not

Old hardware and fittings provide a beautiful finishing touch to the reconstructed house. However, the parts are often worn and covered in paint and it is hard to collect enough pieces of a matching style to do a whole house. Parts or units made at different times by different manufacturers are sometimes not interchangeable. Unless you are a hardware enthusiast, you may want to use some of the fine antique reproductions on the market such as the rim locks and Tudor latch shown here.

This is a Victorian glass knob mounted with a rim lock.

A reproduction cast-steel rim lock. Also shown is an antique porcelain knob of which a reproduction is not yet available.

A reproduction of an English Tudor wrought-iron latch.

A sliding wooden latch on a shed door. This latch slants downward so it cannot work itself loose when the door rattles in the wind.

An antique brass rim lock; a reproduction of this is available.

teeth or rods which slide back and forth across the width. When this device is pressed against a certain shape, the rods move into position according to the contours of the shape; and when taken away, they remain in the exact pattern of that shape, giving you a record of its contours.

The doors, windows, trim and hardware details of a house are every bit as important as the appearance and function of the main shape and structural details. A small, plain, rectangular house can become quite attractive if there is some original detailing of windows, baseboards, etc. It then takes on some warmth and personality. Likewise, the boldest and most splendidly proportioned edifice becomes an incongruous eyesore if the builder's attention has stopped before the finishing touches have been put on.

THE ROOF

The roof design you choose will inevitably be influenced by various factors, such as your finances, available skills and materials, the number and layout of floors in your house, as well as your own personal tastes. You may choose a low-pitched, functional covering which leaves the design accent up to the lower portion of the house or an elaborate, steep-pitched masterwork of elegant dormers and dramatic gable ends. In this section we will pass on some important tips about the whys, wherefores and costs of roof building that we've learned from our own experience. Of course, it's up to you to make a realistic assessment of your own resources before beginning this complicated, expensive and sometimes dangerous task.

The three basic roofing systems are:

cheaper) as from a big manufacturer, and the style and quality is more to our liking. This surprising price variance is probably due to the fact that you are cutting out several middlemen, as well as transportation costs. It also serves to keep small business alive — an admirable, though often futile, effort.

TRIM

Buying proper trim stock from building supply stores is, up to now, next to impossible. Making your own is much

more satisfactory from the point of view of design, personal satisfaction and expense; and it's not as hard as you may think. With a set of molding cutters which fit on a standard table saw, and a bit of time and patience, you can turn out endlessly varied and beautiful trim. A little book of instruction which usually comes with the cutter heads will adequately explain the mechanics of actually doing it. If you want to copy a piece of trim that you have seen and liked you can use a common and inexpensive engineer's template which is shaped like a ruler and composed of small

These interesting eaves trough details present a good alternative to modern-looking plastic or metal troughs. They should be made of cedar or cypress to insure long life.

truss, standard frame and open beam. There are many variations on these basic approaches.

Truss Roofs

Trusses provide the outline of both slopes of the roof (the rafters), connected at their bases by long members (the ceiling joists), which will form the frame for the interior ceiling. The unit is made strong by braces running between the rafters and the ceiling joists in a roughly triangular configuration. The technique of triangulation makes it possible to build house roof trusses entirely of inexpensive, lightweight materials and still maintain adequate support strength.

The individual truss sections are prefabricated on the ground or may be ordered ready-built from building supply stores.

These prefab sections are then hauled up onto the top of the house walls, nailed in place, then covered with plywood or boards.

Whether you build your own trusses or buy them from a shop, you will find this system by far the simplest and least expensive. This type of roof will be finished and insulated even more quickly than you could gather the materials for an open beam roof. Truss roofs are one of the tricks of the trade that make it possible for new housing projects to pop up out of the fields overnight like mushrooms.

Of course you won't be able to use this system if you are building a one-and-a-half storey house, in which the area enclosed by the roof is needed for head room in the upper floors, and you want gable and dormer windows. And it certainly won't work in a one-storey house where you want a cathedral-type ceiling. A good point to note is that one-and-a-half storey construction should only be used if it suits your design or available materials. It is a mistake to use it in the belief that by building only a half-wall upstairs, you will save money, since any small saving will be quickly offset by the extra complication involved in framing and finishing the roof of such a house. The advantages of a truss roof are:

1. Simple initial construction.
2. The interior finish is applied to a straight flat ceiling rather than having to follow the more complicated and larger shape of the entire roof frame, dormers, etc.
3. The majority of the work is done on the ground rather than in place. Working in high places is difficult and time consuming.
4. There is no need to frame soffits as they are provided automatically by the portion

of the ceiling joists which overhang the wall to the exterior.

5. Smaller dimension lumber can be used because the triangular truss configuration is a very strong shape.

6. A minimum of insulation is required because it is applied only to the exact area of the ceiling rather than the whole area of the roof which is obviously larger than the area it covers.

The prime disadvantage of a truss roof system is its inability to satisfy the demands of an intricate, steeply-pitched roof replete with dormers and other exotic complications.

Standard or Custom-Made Frame

This roofing system consists basically of pieces of standard dimension lumber such as 2 × 6s or 2 × 8s placed either 16 inches or 24 inches apart (center to center) so that they form the outline or frame for the main roof, dormers and gable ends. The outside is then sheathed and shingled, and insulation is placed between the frame members. A vapor barrier of plastic or waxed paper is placed on the interior side of the insulation material, and this is covered with the interior finish of plaster or wood. A roof like this will require some skill at layout and fitting, and a fair bit of time, but far less than an open beam roof.

This is the system you will most likely employ if you are steering your design toward an exotic or dramatic roof of dormers and intersecting shapes, bell-cast octagonal towers, etc. The roof of the house in the photo on page 54 is standard frame type.

When you compare a custom-made frame to a basic truss roof, you find it requires more time, more materials, more skill, a greater area to insulate, and more interior finish to complete. This is a good time to remember the designer's truism that "corners cost money" — make your decisions accordingly.

Open or Exposed Beam Frame

Exposed beams show the wonderful lasting beauty of fine-hewn timbers rising into the shadows, and intricate detail to entertain the eye, giving a feeling of openness that is inspiring. But achieving this effect is expensive and time consuming. This method is similar to the standard frame construction roof, except that it uses much larger rafter and collar-tie pieces, for examples 4 × 8s and 4 ×10s spaced about four feet apart. The size and spacing vary with the length of rafter required for each particular house. The exterior is sheathed with two-inch tongue-and-groove planks and the interior left open so the beauty of the wood and workmanship may be fully appreciated.

While an open beam roof is aesthetically pleasing, it has a major disadvantage in that the insulation must go to the outside of the roof. This entails the building of almost another complete roof on the exterior to hold the insulation and shingles. Strapping large enough to accommodate the proper thickness of insulation with a space for ventilation has to be nailed to the outside of the two-inch sheathing, and over this is nailed plywood or boards to nail the shingles to. The thinnest strapping which may be used is at least two-and-a-half inch, in order to accommodate urethane spray insulation, and up to eight inch for fiberglass insulation. Insulation values for

various materials are found in the tables in the appendix.

The large expenditure of time, materials and effort required to build an open beam roof are factors you should consider carefully before deciding to go ahead with this type of roof.

THE MAIN FRAME

If you are fortunate enough to be able to acquire a set of matched hewn beams the right size to suit your needs, it would be a great advantage. Old barn beams are usually unsuitable because of their huge size and weight and the difficulty of finding enough matching pieces to make a whole roof. You may find some barn beams which will be the right size if they are cut in half through their length with a chain saw. The sawn edge can then be hewn, and the whole beam stained to a uniform color. However, the appearance of the hewing which is done this way will not match the original sides. The original hewing was done when the wood was green and a

The builder of this house made the walls from a large quantity of old hewn bridge timbers which he found in the yard of a demolition company.

The short "knee-wall" of this house has been built of frame rather than log, probably because of a shortage of logs of a suitable length. Note that the only full log across the front is actually composed of three separate pieces. To cover the frame knee-wall, the builder has brought the gable end sheathing and roof overhang down very low. This created an unusually large and bulky roof which could have been ungainly had it not been balanced and turned to advantage by the addition of very large dormers.

The finished bathroom of the house on the right.

large chunk of wood was being cut off, and this held the axe against the beam for a longer stroke. In attempting to hew thin pieces from a sawn surface, the axe will glance off more readily giving the final finish the appearance of shorter rougher cuts. If the original surfaces of the beams have a very smooth-hewn finish you will find it better to use an adze rather than a hewing axe to finish the sawn side.

If you don't get old beams for the main roof, you may decide to hew new ones from trees. This would require a good number of straight, wide trees, a good hand with the broad axe and a strong

The rear elevation of the house shown completed on page 106. The roof will be further complicated when the valley rafters, valley jacks and gable ends are added. Because the top floor is only a half-storey, the roof must be built so that the inside may be finished as well as the outside, adding further problems to an already thorny project.

The horizontal lookout rafters over the gable ends provide ready support and nailing for fascia boards, eave boards, gable framing, sheathing and interior finish. They also provide the strength necessary to support a wide overhang. The gable end framing which is not yet installed will support the lookouts.

The large scaffold tower at left underlines the constant problem inherent in the building of multi-storey houses and suggests a reason for the widespread adoption of single-storey ranch-style houses.

Wet ground conditions forced us to build the entire house, basement and all, above the ground, then build a hill around the front and sides so the log front would appear firmly situated on the ground, and the slope of the new hill would channel ground water away from the house.

The earthwork hill, built after this picture was taken, slopes away at the back and the basement becomes the walkout type. Wherever the basement walls protruded from the ground, we switched from cast concrete to frame construction so that thick fiberglass insulation could be used.

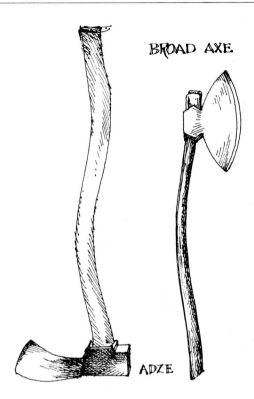

BROAD AXE

ADZE

A closeup of these rafter ends shows curved segments have been cut from the bottom of the rafters and nailed onto the tops to give the final roof a slight bell cast at the eaves. The angled ends of the horizontal collar beams are a clever way of providing nailing for the finish boards and screened vents which will close the area bounded by the rafter faces, wall plate and eventually the roof sheathing. These blocks are necessary in this case because the house will have no soffits and the rafters will be exposed from underneath. Exposed rafter ends also made the carefully sculpted "birds' mouths" desirable. (The bird's mouth is the notch cut from the rafter where it fits over the wall plate.) If they were to be concealed by soffits, a cruder and quicker straight cut would have sufficed.

back. To give you an idea of the time involved, an experienced hewsman should be able to hew four sides of about six 25-footers in a day or so. A novice will be lucky to do one-third as much, and probably won't want to be hewing more than a couple of hours at a time.

You could also order custom-made beams of the desired size from a saw mill, then "dress" the faces of the beams with an adze (see example on page 72), or leave them rough-sawn in a concession to modernity. You can also make the main frame from round logs with one side flattened with an adze, so you can nail on the roof boards. Round log rafters suit a round log building but they would appear incongruous in a hewn log building.

Getting the beams in place will require several strong people and a bit of ingenuity. When we were raising the beams for the house in the photos on pages 72 and 73 (these were green 4 x 10s, up to 24 feet long), we found it was too big a task to pull them up by hand. We had to fasten a good strong pole to the second floor joists so that it would lean against the side wall at about 45 degrees and protrude about six feet beyond the edge of the building. We fastened a block and tackle to the end of this pole, tying one end of the rope to a beam we wanted to lift and the other end to the bumper of a pick-up truck. As the truck drove ahead, the beam was raised to a level just slightly above the top of the house wall. We then swung the beam in over the side and pulled it into the building. We later used the same block and tackle to raise and hold the collar beams while they were being pegged in place.

Once we got the beams up to the second floor, we assembled them in the "A" shape they would finally form by nailing braces onto them, placed one at each end of the building and raised them into place with ropes and poles. After bracing them securely, two men climbed to the top and pulled up one end of the main ridge beam, which had been cut in half for ease of handling. The same was done with the ridge beam at the other end of the house, leaving one end of each section of ridge angling down toward the floor in the middle. We then began building a scaffold under the intersection of the ends of the ridge beams, raising the beams with us as each new section of scaffold was added. By this means, we finally lifted the ends of the ridge beam until they were in their right place forming one long, straight beam. Then the other rafters were put up against it and nailed in place.

THE SHEATHING

For roof sheathing we often use two-inch tongue-and-groove red cedar. Our opinion is that two-inch sheathing is necessary to prevent the boards from being broken or twisted out of place during construction as they are required to span almost four feet between rafters. The thick decking also provides easy nailing for the strapping on the outside. (This thickness is specified in the book, *Architectural Graphic Standards*, listed in the bibliography.)

Cross sections of post-and-purlin roof details showing two different methods.

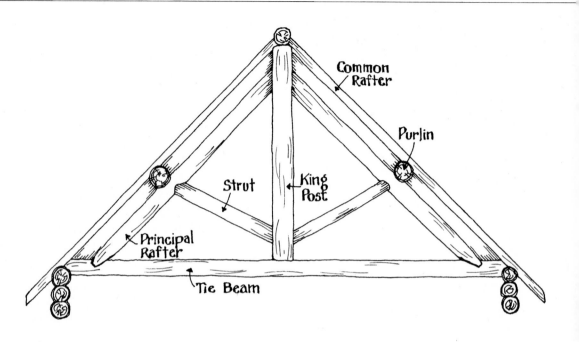

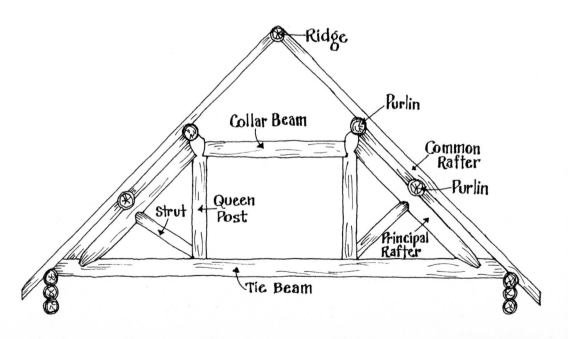

enough timber that they don't need any further support.

A post-and-purlin roof makes use of smaller dimension rafters with approximately the same spacing between them, and these smaller rafters are supported at their mid-points by a purlin. A purlin is

Details of a truss-and-purlin roof at the Fortress of Louisbourg done in the fashion employed by French ship builders in the construction of the original fort.

Obviously the builders put a good deal of thought into this beautiful and complicated juncture of gables, soffits and walls.

This gable end support truss makes possible the very wide overhangs which protect the log walls from the rain.

THE STRAPPING

The thickness of the strapping is decided by the type of insulation you decide to use. Urethane foam takes up the least amount of space, but is also the most expensive. Fiberglass batts are the thickest and the cheapest. Allow a minimum of ¾ inch of additional space so that air can flow around the insulation, to keep it dry (see roof venting section on page 64). The horizontal strapping should not completely fill the gap between the straps running from bottom to top of the roof or they will block the ventilating air from flowing up

between them to the top.

Where the strapping meets the edges of the roof, it must be aligned and trimmed to allow the fascia trim to be nailed on properly later on. When using thick fiberglass insulation, the resulting fascia trim will be very large and heavy looking, which may be an undesirable design element.

Post-and-Purlin Roofs

In the open beam roofing system discussed above, large pieces of timber are used to form A-shaped supports for the roof. These As are made of heavy

a large beam running horizontally from one end of the house to the other, supported on its ends by trusses which sit on top of the gable end walls and by interior trusses if necessary, as in the photo on page 140. This system is also used when the rafters available are not long enough to run from wall plate to ridge beam. Here, the joint formed between the separate pieces of rafter is placed over a purlin for support. This style of roof is also used simply because it is attractive, especially on round log houses. It is the most complicated method of the ones we have discussed.

False Beams

Although a discussion of false beam work will raise disapproval from the purists among us, we feel that we should say a few words about it. We have seen them used so many times by different builders that they have earned at least a mention in any discussion of latter-day log building techniques.

False beams are basically large pieces of wood which are fastened to the underside of a regular standard frame ceiling or roof to give the impression of an open beam main frame. This may at first sound like twice the amount of work and material but there are several instances where this is not the case.

1. If you want beam ceilings where the ceiling will have to incorporate a quantity of plumbing and heating pipes, and wiring for the room above, you may find it easiest to conceal all the mechanical parts in a standard frame; if you want the look of an open frame, you then fasten false beams underneath it.

2. If you are farming out the roof work to someone else because you lack the time or skill to do it yourself, but intend on doing the interior work, you will find false beams a fast and simple method of decorating. Compared to the large costs of time and material required to build true open beams and insulate the roof afterwards, false beams will represent a fair-sized saving.

3. A good matched set of hewn beams are hard to find and even harder to make. If you have some beams to work with that are the wrong size or shape or quality to use in actually supporting part of the building, they may be cut and rearranged so that they would be suitable for false

beams. Large beams may be cut in half down their length, thus doubling their number. The sawn edge is turned against the wall and is not seen. If they are bent or warped a bit it won't matter. Even if they are cracked or broken in the middle they will serve this purpose very well.

We once did an addition for a house in which we wanted to make the interior look like Tudor post-and-beam with plaster between the beams. Rather than taking the time-consuming route of building a true post-and-beam house — with all the problems of finding materials, insulating and making a good seal between the frame work and the edges of the filler panels — we chose the easier method. We built a regular frame structure using 2 × 6 wall studs to give a heavy thick-walled appearance and to hold lots of insulation. On the inside we covered the walls with sheets of gyprock lathing which is used as a base sheathing for a coat of plaster. On the inside of the lath we fastened beams so they could form the outline of the wall posts, wall plates and roof rafters of a heavy timber main frame. The beams we used were unservicable logs from various old partly-decomposed log buildings. They were sawn in half through their thickness to make slabs roughly four inches thick and twelve inches wide, and we turned the sawn side toward the wall surface. Plaster was then put on all the walls between the false beams. The result was what appeared to be a house built from beautiful hand-hewn 12 × 12 timbers, because the edge of the slabs that we put on disappeared into the plaster wall panels just as they would in real timber frame work. No one could tell the difference.

Note: Whether you use screws or nails

to fasten the beams, always drill a hole that will allow the heads to be countersunk and capped with wooden plugs so the fastener heads won't show.

Before putting the beams up, wrap them in thin (cheap) plastic, which can be cut off with a sharp knife after the plaster is in place and before it can completely set. If you don't do this, you are sure to get plaster all over the beams and it is very hard to scrape off later.

LOG PRESERVATION AND FINISH

Building to Prevent Decay

Your log house should be designed to be as dry as possible. Wherever moisture can accumulate, decay-causing fungi, the cause of wood rot, can live. Through the whole construction process attention should be given to not creating any places where water can collect. The areas which are most critical are window and door frames, especially around their lower portions; sill logs and floor joists, exposed end grain; fascia boards; and the lower portion of the logs which is the splash zone.

A wide roof overhang of about 24 inches at the eaves will keep all but the most driving rains off the top portion of the log work. We realize that large overhangs were not at all common in early log construction but we feel that their absence was a serious oversight. Any cracks in the upper quarter of the log's exterior surface will channel water directly to the heart of the log where it may sit and cause decay or continue on to the interior of the building. This problem has caused us considerable grief and we highly recommend a wide roof overhang to combat it. For the same reason, log houses should be built in locations sheltered from wind-driven rain.

The building should be up on a good masonry foundation with a generous slope and ditching to take water away from it. Eavestroughs are also a necessity.

Window and door sills, exposed porches, and sun decks must have enough slope to make water run off. Window and door sills will have a shallow saw cut along the length of their undersides just in from the front edge which causes water to bead up and drop off rather than being held on by surface tension and running inside via the bottom of the sill.

Foundations and roofs have to be ventilated to prevent dampness, as discussed in the section on roof venting.

There are certain woods which are naturally decay resistant: cedars, redwood, white oak, baldcypress, black locust, osageorange, red mulberry, black walnut and yew. These species are recommended for fascia boards, sill logs, and window and door sills. (Door sills are to be hardwood.)

Preservatives

Preservatives prevent decay mostly by killing the fungus which causes it. There are several preservatives which will prevent decay but should not be used for reasons of color and odor. Creosote is a commonly used wood preservative but it will turn the wood black and has a strong and long-lasting odor. The best preservative that we have found is a solution of pentachlorophenol in a light oil base solvent, which is available commercially under several brand names, or can be made up following the formulas given in the appendix. It causes little or no change in the wood color.

Pentachlorophenol is very toxic and should never be used on the inside of a building where it is not necessary. It may be sprayed or brushed on after the logs are up and before the chinking goes in. Protective clothing and gloves should be worn when applying it, since the chemical is absorbed through the skin. This or any other preservative should be reapplied every two years, especially to the splash zone and the log butt ends. You should check the building about once a year, and caulk up any new cracks and crevices, after filling them with wood preservative.

Finishes

INTERIOR

No finish is really necessary on the inside of the logs but there are several which may be used to bring out the grain of the wood or to make the logs easier to clean.

Boiled or raw linseed oil gives wood an attractive lustre without making it shine. It should be thinned by adding 30 percent turpentine and rubbed in well, or it will collect dust. Other conventional penetrating oils, oil stains, or sealers will serve the same purpose, but we do not advise the use of any hard surface finish such as varnish, lacquers or urethanes because when it comes time to refinish these large expanses of rough, irregular log walls, you will have an impossible job of sanding and scraping. However, varnish or urethane are recommended for heavy dirt areas such as doors and windows. These will improve their look, make them easy to clean and prevent ugly cracking and splitting.

EXTERIOR

If left as it is, the exterior of the log work will gradually turn gray. If you want to preserve the natural color of the wood, a penetrating water-repellent preservative or a penetrating pigmented stain may be used. (For formulas, see appendix.)

Preservative-type finishes allow the wood to weather to a natural tan color and prevent the growth of mold which causes graying. It can be brushed on after the logs are up, paying special attention to cracks and end grains. The finish will have to be renewed about every two years as gray spots of mold begin to appear.

Penetrating pigmented stains, which change the natural colour of the wood, may be less attractive than preservative finishes. They do have the added advantage of protecting the wood from discoloration caused by ultraviolet rays of the sun and can last up to ten years (see appendix).

Under no condition should varnish, paint or urethane finishes be used on the exterior logs.

The exterior window and door trim should be treated to prevent it from splitting, discoloring and cracking. We like using paint as it is an excellent preservative, and a bit of color provides a nice accent to the log work. A penetrating stain preservative also works well. Some protection on the exterior fine woodwork is imperative or it will soon crack, begin to hold water and decay. It is a good idea to treat the concealed portions of exterior trim with a preservative before they are nailed up. Urethane will decompose in exterior application and should not be used.

FOUNDATIONS

Several books we have read on the subject of log building describe a system of supporting the house on pillars of stone or blocks. Unless you are building a small, simple house strictly for summertime use, or you live in a very temperate climate, we would caution against building such a second-rate foundation. If you do not want or need a full basement, you should at least build a short wall foundation which completely encloses the area under the house and extends below the frost line. This short wall will provide what is called a "crawl space" under the house. This crawl space is necessary to build and maintain electrical and plumbing systems which are to run under the floor.

If you don't have a continuous perimeter foundation wall, you will be unable to heat under the floors so you will never have warm feet in the winter, no matter how well you insulate the floor. Heat rises, and even though your heaters may produce lots of heat, it will continue to rise — away from the floor. We have found that the temperature can range 30 degrees Fahrenheit from floor level to table height in a house with well-insulated floors that have no source of heat underneath them. The occupants of these houses spend a lot of time in winter with their legs crossed under them, sitting on chairs to keep their feet off the cold floors. The only way to have warm floors is to heat them from underneath. It would be best to have the furnace under the house; but if this is not possible, heat may be driven down under the floor by a fan attached to the furnace. The perimeter foundation wall should be insulated to keep heat from escaping through it. The foundation wall should be insulated on the outside with rigid, extruded foam sheets glued to the wall. Exterior insulation allows heat from the house to enter the foundation wall, thereby decreasing the amount that the concrete will freeze. Also note that all topsoil should be removed from the crawl space area before the house is built and a thin (one-inch) layer of concrete poured to prevent dampness

and musty odors. Note that if the floor is heated from underneath, the floor should *not* be insulated.

If the foundation is not continuous around the house, you are allowing insects and vermin easy access to it. We even know someone whose pigs could not be dissuaded from taking up residence in the pleasant coolness under his house!

Methods

In a good number of cases the builder may find it easier to build the main floor of standard frame rather than of heavy beams. The materials are sometimes easier to get; the amount of time required to get the floor straight and level is reduced; and if you want a finished ceiling in the basement, all the parts of plumbing, heating and wiring can be concealed easily between the floor joists.

If the joists of the floor are extended to come flush with the edge of the foundation, as is the practice with frame houses, and the logs are set on the joists, the edges of the floor system will be visible between the log work and the foundation. This area may be covered over later with boards, but we think that doing this creates an undesirable visual effect. To overcome this, we have developed a system which is illustrated on the opposite page. The same theory can be followed when building a stone foundation.

If heavy beams are to be used to support the floor instead of a standard frame, the beams may sit in pockets or openings in the top of the foundation wall. Their ends should be wrapped in plastic to keep moisture from the foundation from entering the wood. The beams may also be set in pockets in the first course of logs but if you do this, you will have to build a higher log wall to get the same head

clearance. We won't go into detail about building foundations as there are already some competent books on the subject. But we would like to emphasize what we have found to be the critical points in the construction of foundations.

In theory, a foundation should be perfectly square, but if it is out $1/2$ inch or so, don't worry. You can compensate for this quite easily in the woodwork which comes afterwards. However, if the foundation top is not *level*, you can expect endless trouble throughout the rest of the project, because the foundation is the reference point for many measurements made when building the walls and the roof.

Make sure the foundation walls are heavy enough. Modern split-level houses can get away with using blocks as small as eight inches thick because the exterior grade only comes half way up the wall and the rest is left exposed. A log house would look terrible with concrete blocks sticking out of the ground in this way, and you will want to bring the grade line to within six inches of the top of the wall to allow for this. The greater weight of fill required here calls for thicker walls. The unsupported length of a foundation wall — that is, the length between corners and intersecting walls — also affects the thickness of wall required. Check your local building codes to find out what will be needed in your design.

Lay your weeping pipe, which drains the area around the foundation, at the same level as the concrete footings which the walls sit on — not against the walls themselves. Put lots of gravel (about eight inches of it) over them to protect them from being crushed when backfilling or from becoming plugged later with sediment. Weeping pipe and the gravel for under the basement floor are most easily put in after the footings are done and before the walls go up. Great care should be taken in installing these drainage pipes and providing a proper outlet for them, since repairing them later is a nightmarish task. If these drains don't work properly, water will build up against the basement wall and force its way in.

Coating the outside of the foundation wall with 6 mil plastic sheeting, laid over the necessary tar coating, is highly recommended.

If the ground around your site is heavy, sticky clay, we recommend that you go to the extra trouble of trucking in sandy soil to use as backfill against the wall. Heavy clay has absolutely no drainage, and will hold water against the wall where it can find its way in. Also, if a heavy rain comes after the wall has been backfilled with clay, the loose dirt may turn into a heavy, running mess which can in some cases push the wall down — certainly a situation to be avoided.

Excavating

The first thing to do when the excavator arrives is to pile up all the topsoil in a location well away from the site. Wherever excavated dirt is piled, the topsoil will be lost, so take the topsoil off the entire area where the house will stand, and at least 15 feet around it. If you don't do this, you will have to truck in new soil before you can get plants and grass to grow again. Again, that will be another expenditure, because topsoil is very expensive. Pile the dirt from the excavation where it will not interfere with the concrete and gravel trucks that will be coming in.

If your foundation wall is to be, say, eight feet high, do not dig an eight-foot-deep hole to put it in. The excavation walls would be very tall, increasing the danger of collapse. You would also be faced with the problem of getting rid of a huge pile of dirt. Instead, dig a hole that is four or five feet deep, and use the dirt from the hole to build a hill around the basement once it is in place. This has the double advantage of providing a good slope which helps water run away from the house.

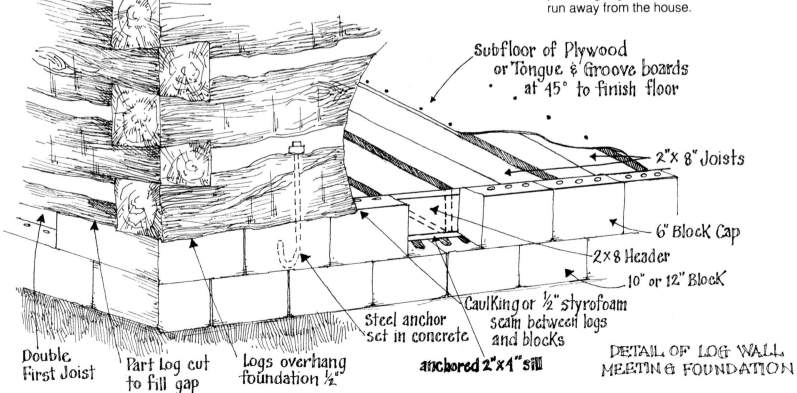

Subfloor of Plywood or Tongue & Groove boards at 45° to finish floor

2" x 8" Joists

6" Block Cap

2 x 8 Header

10" or 12" Block

Caulking or ½" styrofoam seam between logs and blocks

Steel anchor set in concrete

anchored 2"x4" sill

Double First Joist

Part Log cut to fill gap

Logs overhang foundation ½"

DETAIL OF LOG WALL MEETING FOUNDATION

It would be a fatal mistake to place the house so low in the ground that it is lower than the surrounding landscape, thus creating your own private swamp. It is best to make any error in favor of having it too high as more dirt can be banked around it later.

A little mathematical work will tell you how much dirt will come out of a hole of a certain depth and how big a hill it will make around the house. Don't make too small and abrupt a hill or it will look ridiculous. Dig slowly and carefully as you reach the bottom of the hole. If you dig too far, you cannot fill it back in to the right level. This loose dirt will not support the footings. Footings must always be laid on undisturbed ground.

Later on, when you have finished the roof of the house, put your eavestroughs on as soon as you can, or the roof will channel large quantities of water onto the freshly-disturbed ground around the house, causing undesirable eroding and possible leakage. If this saturated, loose dirt freezes for the winter, it may heave the top few feet of the wall.

Be sure to plug up any holes that are to be made in the foundation under the surface to bring in water pipes or electric wires. Plumbers and electricians are notoriously lax in this respect. We built one house in which the plumbers failed to plug the hole where oil came in from a buried tank. We also didn't put eavestroughs on the house right away. That spring we were treated to the sight of antique furniture standing in water a couple of inches above the carpeting. We couldn't find the leak because the water runs along inside the block work before it finds its way out, making it impossible to find where it was coming in. We had to move a hundred tons of dirt from the back of an eighty-foot

house to find that one leak the plumbers insisted they had plugged.

Stone Foundations

It has been our experience that building a stone foundation is a long and back-breaking process requiring months of work for the inexperienced builder. It provides an end product which is in no way superior to blocks — and it gets buried out of sight anyway. Unless you really know what you are getting into, avoid building a stone foundation.

A silent testimonial to the strength of log walls. This foundation collapsed several years ago, but the walls have not.

INSULATION

In the last several years the cost of fuel oils and the awareness of the need to conserve them have increased greatly. As a result, the practice of using 2- x 4-inch dimension lumber, 16 inches on center, for all wall sections, gable ends, etc., is gradually being replaced by the use of 2- x 6-inch members, 24 inches on center, so that thicker insulation may be used. The

A high level of ground water forced this builder to locate the basement wall top well above grade and build a palisade around it later. The steep location and the height of the house made construction very difficult as the only access was from below.

use of larger members spaced wider apart gives the same wall strength as the smaller pieces, placed closer together. The actual cubic volume of lumber used is increased a bit, but this is balanced by the fact that time to install the pieces is reduced. Two-by six-inch construction makes the walls thicker. This is noticable around the doors and windows, the effect enhancing the feeling of substantial solidness of the house.

Urethane Spray Foam Insulation

This recently-developed plastic insulator is available in rigid sheets, but can also be used in spray form, creating a perfectly seamless fit, eliminating heat loss through cracks. The spray nozzle blends two separate streams of chemicals as they are applied to a surface. The two chemicals react and begin to foam up within 45 seconds. The foam hardens forming a multi-cell plastic with wonderful insulating properties. The foam adheres to wood so well that when broken away, it leaves a $1/8$- to $1/4$-inch coating stuck to the wood. It is virtually windproof, and of all the commercially available insulators, it has the highest insulation value per inch of thickness.

Near any major center and in most agricultural areas where cold storage construction is required, professional suppliers can be found who will come with all the equipment and chemicals in a truck and spray it in for you. Urethane foam is also available in disposable back pack units for use in remote areas. We have used these to insulate the chinking in log buildings with very satisfactory results — after a little practice. However, the expense of the portable packs makes them impractical for more extensive use.

All things considered, we have found urethane foam to be the best product to use to insulate chinking courses. It has a high insulation value, and will seal with the wood forming a wind-proof barrier, which will stop drafts finding their way through any cracks in the mortar. Used with seasoned logs where little movement is expected, it is excellent for sealing around doors and windows.

The chemical reactions which create the foam are very critical to heat and humidity — if you do not follow carefully the manufacturer's specifications, the foam you get can fall far short of your expectations. Although there may not be any visible problem immediately, you may discover that the foam has lost most of its insulation value. In some cases, it may harden later (curing time is 28 days) to the point where it turns to powder.

The foam comes in different densities which vary widely in cost and thermal efficiency. When shopping around, make sure that the foams you are comparing have the same insulation value.

A word of caution: Urethane foam will burn when raised to a very high temperature. In burning it produces a poisonous cyanide gas. It must be covered with at least $3/8$ inches of plaster or an equivalent material. Using it between the courses of mortar in the chinking is acceptable because a urethane-insulated house unfortunate enough to catch fire will be long gone before the flames of a fire have reached the foam.

Pay careful attention to the manufacturer's advice regarding protective masks and clothing. Although the chemicals are not poisonous themselves, except when burned, they still have some of the other unpleasant properties for which plastic is becoming infamous.

Polystyrene (Styrofoam)

Polystyrene comes in rigid sheets of various thicknesses. There are two distinct types with very different properties and the two should not be confused when comparison shopping. The first and most common is white, sometimes having blue spots of fire retardant in it. It is made by molding together expanded beads of polystyrene, and is sometimes referred to as bead board. The second type is usually blue and is made by extruding a solid sheet of polystyrene. This extruded type will be found to have considerably better thermal resistance properties, or R-value, than the first type, and is of course more expensive per thermal resistance unit. The use of more expensive extruded foam is mandatory if the insulation is going to be exposed to dampness.

Fiberglass

Fiberglass requires more insulation thickness to achieve the same insulation value than the foam type does. It is currently the most common insulator because it performs as well as the plastic insulators when applied thickly enough and is generally cheaper per thermal resistance unit.

Vapor Barrier

All insulation is covered on the inside, or heat side, by a thin 2 to 5 mil plastic or treated paper covering. This is used to prevent moisture from the inside of the house from passing into the insulation, thereby making it wet and reducing its value; so leaving the vapor barrier out will significantly increase heat loss. Never use a vapor barrier on both sides of the insulation as severe condensation may occur between the layers, soaking the insulation and making it virtually useless.

Note: Old houses are dry in the winter because:

1. Dry outside air is filtering in freely around doors, windows and foundation sill.
2. Water vapor migrates freely through walls that have no vapor barrier and this creates the need to constantly add new moisture.

In new houses with complete vapor barriers and no drafts (i.e., weather stripping around all openings), the humidity isn't diluted with dry outside air, and the moisture can't go through the walls. The result is that the most common problem is too much humidity trapped in the house as a result of living activities. The best solution is a heat exchanger that uses outgoing moist air to heat incoming dry air. This is the only way to stop excess condensation on windows, etc., without adding a greater load to the heating system. A dehumidifier or simply the opening of a door or window are equally effective ways, but they waste more energy and are increasingly expensive.

Ventilation

All insulated areas must be ventilated. The difference in temperature between the inside and outside surfaces of a wall will cause condensation or dew to form inside the wall. This may cause wet rot, as well as make the insulation ineffective. Tightly-sealed areas such as roofs and basements can create ideal conditions for dry rot as well.

Vents of a size equal to one square foot per 300 square feet of ceiling area should be made both along the soffits at the bottom of the roof and at the peak of the roof. This will allow air to circulate through the roof, over the top of the insulation. We have seen unvented attics completely coated in the winter with hoar frost and ice — not the best of situations! For the same reasons, basements should always be supplied with windows for cross ventilation. While doing renovations to a house whose basement had been sealed tightly for several years, we found some of the main beams so badly dry rotted that huge chunks could be pulled off the beams by hand. To the eye these beams appeared perfect but the dry rot fungus had turned them to dust. In the case of a house with a crawl space rather than a basement, vents should be made with sliding wooden covers which can be opened in summer and closed in winter. All types of vents should be covered with bug screens — for obvious reasons.

In standard frame construction, the roof is vented in the cold roof area above the collar ties or ceiling joists. In open beam design, venting becomes a bit more difficult. The peak of the roof may be left open a few inches and a small secondary roof built on top extending down the roof about 18 inches on either side and about two inches above it. It should be fitted with bug screens as well.

Another way to provide ventilation is to leave the butt ends of the insulation strapping cut square on the ends forming a V-shaped channel inside the peak of the roof. On a large house, small cupolas or vent stacks must be made once or twice along the peak of the roof to supplement the openings in the gable ends.

As a useful rule of thumb, always construct a wall that is as tight and moisture proof on the inside as possible. Outside surfaces do not have to be draft proof and in fact air infiltration on the outside surfaces of insulation may be very beneficial in removing moisture that has seeped through from the living area.

Wiring

Keep electrical wiring away from log work as much as possible. Standard frame partitions are the best place for it. Electrical codes vary from area to area, so consult your local code before beginning.

For chinked logs, run the wiring inside the chinks before the mortar is applied. Outlet boxes can be cut into the log faces or mortared into the chinks. For chinkless logs, you can either pre-drill the logs during installation, or run the wiring up the corners in small channels chiseled out and mortared over later.

This roof vent is made from a regular louvred shutter (available at most building stores). The soffits and fascia boards are western red cedar which will resist decay in problem spots such as behind the eaves troughs.

The Order of Work

A flexible list to help the log builder decide what to do when.

1. Locate site.
2. Design, plan and estimate.
3. Make up lists (schedules) of parts and materials.
4. Build road.
5. Clear site. To be done in the spring or fall; no bugs, less undergrowth.
6. Drill well (to make water available during construction).
7. Have temporary electric power service hooked up.
8. Excavate.
9. Put in footings.
10. Drainage tile is most easily installed now.
11. Pour gravel for the basement floor.
12. Build foundation wall; parge and waterproof.
13. Backfill foundation and do rough grading.
14. Build fireplace (rough). This can be done later with careful planning of framing.
15. Erect main support beams and first floor frame and subfloor.
16. Pour the basement floor. The first floor protects it from rain and sun damage during drying.
17. Build log walls.
18. Install subfloor for second level. If the second floor boards are the solid plank type, which serve as the finished floor as well as the ceiling for the level below, wait until the roof is on to avoid water damage to floor. Sand the underside of the planks before installing them — it's too hard later.
19. Frame and shingle roof.
20. Install soffits, gable sheathing, any exterior sheathing and fascia trim.
21. Apply any exterior stains or preservatives to woodwork. If done now, they may be sprayed on.
22. Install eaves troughs now to prevent erosion and splash damage to woodwork.
23. Install stairs and cover to protect.
24. Do interior framing.
25. Install windows, doors and trim. Cover sills to protect them. This is done now so the chinking will seal with the trim.
26. Rough in heat ducts and furnace.
27. Install septic tank and tile bed, and dig trenches for plumbing and hydro into house.
28. Rough in plumbing, and pressure test. Cover bath tub to protect.
29. Rough in wiring and service panel. The mechanical systems often conflict and compete for space inside the walls; therefore, the least flexible ones are done first. Wiring must not run near pipes or ducts. Ducts cannot change direction to avoid pipes or wires, etc.
30. Do exterior chinking, insulate it, and put in the interior wire lath.
31. Finish fireplace. (Very messy if left until later on.)
32. Insulate and install vapor barrier.
33. Put up drywall and paint on primer coat. Temperature must be maintained above 55°F (13°C.) for taping and finishing; this may require that the furnace be turned on.
34. Interior chinking (done last to mate with drywall which is scribed to fit at intersections with logs).
35. Install finished floors.
36. Do interior trim and cabinets.
37. Sand, stain and finish the trim and floors. Trim is sanded after cutting and before installing.
38. Install plumbing fixtures.
39. Paint.
40. Install electric and plumbing finish trim.
41. Finish grade and landscaping.
42. Move in now, not before — not even a little bit!

A restored hewn log house at Black Creek Pioneer Village.

The same urge that makes people strip the paint off an old table or replace the broken spindles of a Boston rocker leads them to reclaim the many old log farm houses that dot the rural areas of North America. Living in an old log house is the ultimate in antique collecting — it's certainly the largest antique you're likely to find!

The first step in reconstructing a log house is to find a set of good hewn logs, or two or three sets if you are planning a big house. The easiest, but most expensive, source is a dealer who is in the business of searching them out in rural areas and reselling them. Make sure you pick a dealer with a reputation for backing up what he sells. Get some references from previous customers and write out a

detailed letter of agreement to be signed by both parties. If you can't actually inspect the building from which the logs will be (or have been) taken, you should at least see a photograph of it before it was dismantled. This will help you to see what it is you are buying as far as the size of the logs and quality of the corner work is concerned. This can also help you to get over the shock that often comes when the building is actually delivered to your site. Stacked in a pile on the ground, the logs often don't look as if they'll *ever* become a house — epecially not the house you're planning!

Because old log buildings have been exposed to the weather for up to a hundred years or more, they are bound to

Removal of the siding on this house revealed a solid set of logs. Sandblasting removed the whitewash.

need some logs replaced. A dealer should be able to provide the correct size and shape replacement logs as soon as they are needed. We can't emphasize this aspect of reconstructing old buildings too much, since getting replacement logs can be as hard as getting the building itself.

FINDING YOUR OWN LOGS

If you have the time to spare, an adventurous spirit, and a good vehicle, you can try to locate a set of logs on your own. Several years ago, we used to be able to pick up an old log house in exchange for simply removing it and cleaning up the rubble left behind after dismantling. But that doesn't happen anymore. Placing

advertisements for old log buildings in local newspapers doesn't work quite as well as it used to either, because of increased competition, but it might be worth a try. If you try this, make it clear in the ad that you are *not* a dealer.

Though tramping around the country backroads is a wonderful way to spend a summer, you have to be organized so you can find the log building you want. To accomplish this, get state or provincial survey maps of an area you think is a promising one. The buildings marked on these maps may not be visible from the road, since some of them were built back on the lot in the days when concession roads were in no better condition than the farm driveway — or altogether

nonexistent. Look for an overgrown path leading from the concession road off into the woods. The houses that were visible from the main road will probably already have been seen and bought. If you find an abandoned building that looks promising, leave your vehicle at the gate and walk in, or better still, ask neighboring farmers about it, always making sure to show your good intentions. Looking for a log building is a good way to meet rural people who are generally warm and friendly. These people are usually proud of their knowledge of the area, and are often great conversationalists. If you are patient, you can get the history of every house and milkshed within fifty miles — when it was built, by whom, and how many times it was

This is what happens to a house with a leaky roof in only a few short years. Three years ago this building appeared to be in fairly good condition except for a bad roof, but dripping water seems to have dissolved all the wood in its path. Decomposition must have already been invisibly underway.

moved. Polite questioning might even reveal an uncle or cousin who has a log building for sale on his back forty. At any rate, you may spend some very pleasant weekends talking and drinking tea with fascinating people you might otherwise never have met.

One very important thing to remember in your search for an old log building is that they do not always *look* like log buildings. Logs went out of style years ago as a building material for houses, and many log dwellings had their rough-hewn exteriors covered up with clapboard, tarpaper, or aluminum siding. At first glance, such a house looks like an ordinary frame house, but if you look closely at the walls around

the windows and see that they are really thick, chances are that it is a log house. Another point to watch out for is window construction in the gable ends of a log building. These windows are usually higher than the eaves, so that the windows didn't have to be notched down into the logs, whereas in most frame houses, the windows were built at a lower and more convenient level.

These covered-up log buildings can be especially good finds because the siding has very often kept the logs underneath from getting weathered and pitted. It's an exhilarating feeling to watch the old siding being ripped off a building that looks like a run-down tarpaper shack, and see rich, yellow pine logs revealed underneath.

After you have located a building that you like and discovered that you might be able to purchase it, you have to determine whether or not it is in good condition, and it is hard to be objective about this sometimes. When you first come upon an old log house, you can be carried away by

Careless patch jobs such as this can lurk concealed beneath board siding. This one would be fairly easy to repair during reconstruction by enlarging the height of the windows and replacing the filler logs between them.

Overleaf, left: This is the living room of the house shown on the front cover. The spiral stairs climb to an ornate balcony which connects the second floors of the opposite ends of the house. (The railing originally came from an old church.) A hewn timber main frame supports the roof which rises to a height of twenty-seven feet.

Overleaf, right: This end view of the same house shows a greenhouse and a bell tower. The house is laid out in a long and narrow manner, like a chateau, to give it as much exposure as possible to the south and to the nearby lake. In its construction, we used four log houses and a log armoury, parts from a schoolhouse, a firehall and a church, and over one hundred tons of stone. The owner collected the antique pieces himself over a period of several years. The house represents more than seven man-years of work in assembly alone.

the exhilaration of discovery: the horizontal lines of the interwoven logs, the tilted angles of a sagging roof, a whole assortment of hand-hewn textures and strange smells. But soon you must pay attention to the more practical aspects of your find, and ask three important questions:

1. Is the roof in good repair? A leaking roof will let water drip onto the top (plate) logs and seep down the wooden pegs that are driven into them, as well as collecting in the rafter notches, causing rot.
2. What kind of foundation has it been built on? If the bottom (sill) logs have not been kept off the ground, or are banked up with dirt, they will have long ago decayed. A basement is a good sign, usually indicating that the original builder has done a good job on the rest of the building, as well as keeping the logs dry and solid.
3. Are there any irregularities in the log-work? Watch for blocks of wood in the dovetail corners, a tell-tale sign that some bygone cornerman in a hurry has cut a notch too small and inserted a block of wood to bring it up to the proper height.

Appearing solid and serene in its natural setting, this pine log house turned out to be a lesson in wood decomposition. The logs appeared nearly perfect as the building was dismantled, but as they were being handled during reconstruction, several of them literally turned to dust. It taught us that the last part of a pine log to decompose is a thin layer of the outer surface and that diligent probing with an ice pick is a mandatory check. The massive logs under the windows were the ones most affected. Only through extensive reorganization and replacement were we able to save the building and make it part of the chateau pictured on page 73.

Some long logs may be spliced together or an unwanted window sealed up with short logs, thus ruining the continuity of the wall.

These are not insurmountable problems by any means, but you should know what you are getting yourself into. Replacing logs and correcting unsightly defects takes time and money, although any defects that you do find can be turned into bargaining points when discussing the final price.

You should examine the whole building very carefully, log by log. There are two simple tools for this purpose: an ice pick for probing, and a heavy hammer or steel mallet for sounding the logs for hollow (rotten) spots. Use your ice pick to probe the cracks and knotholes, and to check for cavities or punky (spongy) wood. Poke into the dovetail corner face, which is the end of the log and is all end grain. These are often spongy and pitted and you will want to see how far back into the wood this deterioration goes.

Use your mallet to hit the log and hear what it sounds like. It shouldn't rattle or sound hollow, the hammer should bounce back, and the log should reverberate with a high-pitched tone. You may find hollow areas under the windows where water has run down the sides of the upright window frames and kept the logs damp. This dampness sets up conditions that are most favorable for growth of the fungi that cause decay, and it can form a cavity in the log that is invisible from the outside, so make sure you sound the logs under the windows with your hammer. Watch for white or yellow stains around knotholes — this can be dry rot. Determine its extent by probing into it with your ice pick. If you see ants coming out of a crevice, investigate

further for hollowed-out spots. Dark or discolored patches can indicate the presence of moisture and should be checked closely.

Look closely at the chinking. If the mortar was put in wrongly, that is, if it extends beyond the upper drip ledge, (see illustration on page 108), water can trickle down behind and underneath it. Pull some chinking out and check behind it. Be wary of any large, long lateral cracks on the outside face of the log. These can funnel water into the heart of the log if they are on the upper half of the log face and

Overleaf, left (clockwise): A bedroom in the same chateau-style house, showing the open beam roof.

This house appears so natural and settled that it is hard to imagine that it was moved here and rebuilt only a few short years ago.

Left end view of house on page 67, showing imaginative octagon-shaped window.

Splendid design and artful construction distinguish this example of the newly-revived long log construction method. Green logs were used in its construction, necessitating careful planning of plumbing, heating, fireplace, stairs, windows and doors so that none of the parts would be destroyed or damaged as the building was settling down almost six inches during drying.

Overleaf, right (clockwise): The kitchen of the house on the cover. The glazed tile floor is laid on one-and-half inches of wire-reinforced concrete, which was poured over a 5/8-inch plywood sub-floor.

This log drive shed with an apartment on top serves the house shown on page 81. The large windows were partly inspired by the fact that the original logs had been cut away to allow entry by farm equipment before the building was moved to its present location.

should be probed. Keep an eye out for logs with a natural growth spiral of the grain, which can easily be detected because any cracks, splits, or checks will appear in a long spiral pattern, as though the log has been twisted. These are often found to be rotten.

Look carefully at any points where additions or porches have been or are now joined to the building. These additions, especially their roofs, will channel water onto the log walls.

If the walls of the house are marred by whitewash, or other discolorations, you need not reject the house, as sandblasting can restore such logs to their original color.

It is important to take your time and weigh the pros and cons of any particular building. Of course, you will want the building to be right, but if you are tired of looking, if you've just been bitten by a wasp, and the owner is standing there ready to sell, you just might buy on impulse.

We don't want to convey the impression that defects cannot be corrected, however. Rot under the windows can be rectified by making the windows bigger. And if you find a house with a rotten wall or door section, you can put in a fireplace or a big bay window, or have it as a common wall to an addition. A rotten sill or wall log can be replaced, if a new one can be found to match it. Wall plates, because they are square, can be replaced by barn beams which are often more readily available than house logs. Use your imagination to see what can and cannot be done, without underestimating the time and materials required to do it — and be realistic.

If you have the good fortune to have more than one building to choose from,

avoid being swayed in your decision by the parts and pieces such as floor boards, fancy trim, etc., that might come with a house. These are only icing on the cake, and can be obtained elsewhere or reproduced. If the cost of labor required to restore these pieces is considered, their inclusion with the building represents little or no saving over the cost of new material. It is the quality of the log work which is your prime consideration as it is the only element which cannot be altered in the construction of the building. We know one log dealer who justifies his high prices by claiming that his houses are sold as complete buildings, ready to just be put back together rather than merely being sets of logs. Given the condition of the parts of a hundred-year-old house, we say that this claim is most often bunk.

In your search for a house, you don't have to confine yourself to buildings that were used as dwellings. Granaries and horse stables were usually hewn so that they could be sealed easily, and these can make excellent homes, either alone or combined with other log buildings to give added floor space. If you can find a utility building in good condition, this will provide you with replacement logs you are sure to need in the reconstruction of your building.

Round barn logs usually look pretty rough with their hanging bark, but if you can get your hands on a good set and hew them flat you will have a good set of logs to work with. And remember, barns don't usually have windows, so you can cut yours anywhere you want them.

There is a lot of speculation about exactly why the logs were hewn at all, and to be honest, we have never heard a single explanation that would explain it satisfactorily. It could be that it made the logs lighter and easier to handle, or that

cutting off the rot-susceptible sap wood on the outside down to the more rot-resistant heartwood made the extra work worthwhile. Another reason for hewing is that a round log will allow rainwater to run along the curved surface of the bottom of the log and get behind the mortar. A square log has a sharp edge which functions as a drip ledge (discussed on page 108), causing the water to drop off before it gets to the mortar.

Hewn logs are easier to trim around openings and they also provide a flat surface to attach cabinets and other bits of interior finish. But probably the most pertinent reason for hewing the logs flat was to make them appear proper and finished in the eyes of an old world immigrant accustomed to the appearance of fine brick and stone work.

Antique logs are a good building material. They have been seasoned (dried) by being stacked up for many years, and they are a large size you usually can't get anymore — in this age of managed tree plantations. After you have seen a couple of log buildings in good condition, you will be impressed by the skill and craftsmanship our ancestors put into their log work. Though the arts of hewing and dovetail notching are currently undergoing a revival, the old-timers who built those buildings were really master craftsmen in the true sense of the word, and these examples of their work are truly worth saving.

A BUILDING'S HISTORY

The time between your purchase of a building and when it is dismantled provides you with a unique opportunity to study the past. What you have is a mini-museum of early North American history. You can tell a lot about the age of a building and the people who built it just by its design and method of construction. Dovetail notching was preferred by German and Irish immigrants. The keying found in Pennsylvania log buildings was also a German innovation. Scribing and saddle-notching are Scandinavian methods of construction.

Dig around and find out what kinds of nails were used. Hand-forged nails are of course the earliest kind, then came cut nails, and then around the turn of the century came the wire nails we use today. The use of these different types of nails can help you locate and date any additions that were done to your house. Additions to the house often correspond to additions to the family and all this can be checked with county records.

Take a careful look at the window and door frames. Have they been pegged or nailed? What about the roof and floor boards — do they have the rough, irregular, chiseled look of hand-worked wood (indicating an earlier period) or the saw marks of the mills that came later? Even the different types of saw marks can indicate a particular time period, or the financial sutuation of the builder. The angled, irregular up-and-down strokes of the hand saw came before the circular marks of the water- or gas-driven saw mill blade. Often newspapers were used to plug up drafty cracks and seams, or even wrapped around beams and rafters for insulation. If you look at the dates on these newspapers, you can make a fairly accurate guess as to the age of the house — and often they are fascinating reading! They might also give you an indication of when the coldest weather occurred. An amateur archeologist, and that's what you'll be, can reconstruct the lives of the previous tenants by sifting through the junk that accumulated in cellars and attics — not to mention the fun you can have reading old letters you may find.

We are part owners of a very old log house on some cooperatively owned land in Ontario. This house has a gap in the floor boards that is two inches wide, running right down the middle of the first floor with corresponding nail holes in the beam above it. Obviously this already small room had been bisected at one time — but why? We puzzled over this oddity for years until we found out, while searching through the county records, that the original builder back in 1861, had willed half the kitchen and one bedroom on the south side of the house to his daughter and the rest of the house to his son. The daughter would also get a cow if she ever married. The two siblings had complied with their father's wishes and split the house right down the middle. One half of the house had about eight layers of flowery wallpaper, and the other half none!

DISMANTLING

You don't need to learn many extra skills to dismantle a log building, but you have to be very careful. There is something so satisfying about tearing a building apart that many people tend to get a little carried away in a frenzy of destruction. It's a good idea to get a crew of friends together for a tearing down party. When we do this, we often have to ask everyone to slow down once or twice, and they stare back at us with glazed eyes, sweat streaking their dust-covered faces. Make sure everyone wears dust masks, hard hats and steel-toed (and soled) construction boots for safety. The only tools you are likely to need are claw-hammers, rope, a chain saw, wrecking bars (crow-bars), ladders and sledge hammers. Actually, a twenty-pound wooden sledge hammer, called a circus hammer, is handy because its large striking surface will knock out a whole section of stud wall by shearing the nails outwards, whereas a metal sledge hammer will just put a hole in the wall.

Try to salvage as much useful material as possible to save on future costs and to preserve the original character of the building. Start by removing all the baseboards, the door and window trimming, hand-turned banisters, molding and other kinds of trim which you have decided will be useful later.

Old staircases that are worn with the passing of many feet can be a lovely addition to your house if they're not too deeply dished. However, in most

Overleaf, left: This finely-worked oak staircase serves the house on the opposite page.

Overleaf, right (clockwise): The front view of this house, featured in the design section, belies its real size.
The master bedroom of the same house, with stuccoed walls and ceiling, and a brick fireplace.
The living room continues the feeling of a colonial-period gentleman's residence.

Removing Tongue & Groove Boards

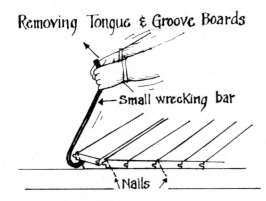

— Small wrecking bar

Nails

When removing tongue-and-groove boards, always begin at the tongue side so the nails will be pulled out at the same angle that they were driven in. Use a wrecking bar with a very short hook to pull the board forward and upward. Short pulls on the bar rather than one long pull seem to encourage the tongue and groove to separate more easily and with less breakage.

cases the second floor height of the reconstructed house will be larger than the original, or at least different, due to the replacement of logs and to the method used in starting a house on a new foundation. If the second floor height is exactly one tread rise larger, a new tread can be added under the old stairs. But if the height is only half a rise different, the stairs will be unusable.

Sometimes, entire interiors are paneled in narrow slats of intricately-patterned

The L-shaped house. The right hand portion of this house is the original. The logs of the addition on the left butt up against it, and the windows are composed of larger sheets of glass, indicating a later period.

tongue-and-groove wood, and, if it has not been painted, this is worth saving along with the wainscoting and flooring.

Roof boards are not usually worth very much because of shingle nail holes and rot. Rafters probably won't have the strength to conform to present building code standards or the thickness and correct spacing to take modern insulation, so you likely won't want to keep them. We are referring here to the small, round pole rafters which were often hewn only from one side — the top. However, if you do find some good, square hewn rafters that you want to save and reuse, you can duplicate them by hewing additional ones and putting them closer together if necessary to meet present building code standards. Rafters that you are not going to use can be sold or traded to defray some of your other costs.

Always start at the top of a building and work down when dismantling a log building. Take the roof boards off first and then if there are any ceiling boards or plaster, you can bang this down from above with your hammer. Save the floors for last, but when you do take them up, rip up the floor of the second storey first, and bang down the ceiling plaster, as you did with the roof. Keep all the rubble away from the outside walls of the building so that the logging truck (or whatever dismantling device you will be using) can get close to the building.

If your building has a basement, remove a few feet of flooring on one side of the house and push the rubble into the basement where it can be burned later, during the following winter. When working on a building that has sat undisturbed for a long time, you can expect a few surprises. You'll want to watch out for wasps' nests in the walls, and in some

The hydraulic log loader swings a giant club to knock the rafters from a decrepit barn being dismantled for spare logs— expedient but unsafe.

Overleaf, left: The simplicity of this old log house is complimented by the beauty of the surrounding countryside.

Overleaf, right: We built this barn so that a tractor and wagon could drive straight through on both upper and lower levels. The photograph on page 96 shows the logs being raised by a crane, a one-day job thanks to the good condition of the logs. (With most of the houses that we have reconstructed, one to three weeks were necessary for a set of logs to be repaired and raised.)

parts even rattlesnakes. During one dismantling, we were constantly being showered with slumbering bats that had nested in the hollow ceilings! There are some heart-rending moments, when you break open a wall and find a bird's nest full of chirping little balls of fluff. Once, when we were taking down a house in Quebec, we uncovered a flying squirrel's nest. We carefully removed the young away from the building, but the mother kept running up the walls and diving at us. She had five strong men stopped cold for hours!

Numbering the Logs

Before you take the logs down, you must remember to number them. This is an extremely important step, and it is your last chance to do it. While the building is still standing, it looks so naturally constructed, but when you've taken it apart, the pile of logs on the ground looks like a giant jig-saw puzzle of logs and notches in various sizes, impossible to put together again without great difficulty if they haven't been numbered. By numbering the logs, you can put this puzzle back together again fairly easily.

Yellow clay bricks covered this fine old log house for years before it was finally moved and rebuilt. The men are seen here removing the buck plates around the windows and doors which will leave the filler logs between the window and door unsupported. They should be wearing hard hats.

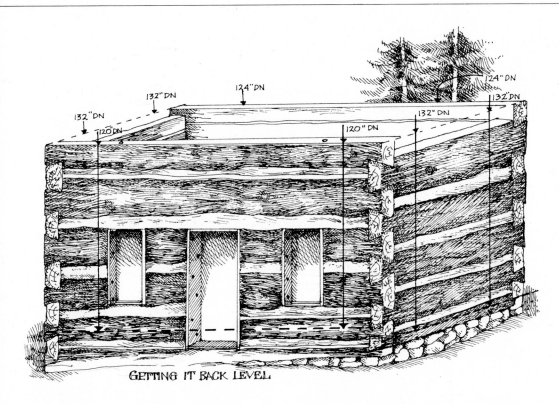

GETTING IT BACK LEVEL

All notations should be made from a fixed reference point, such as outside the building facing the front, so that left and right will have a constant point to relate to.

Number the logs from bottom to top (F1, F2, F3, B1, B2, B3, etc.) by nailing a numbered steel plate on the dovetail end of the log it belongs to. Make sure that all the plates are on the same end of the wall and that they are all nailed on vertically. This will help you determine which is the inside and which is the outside face of the log. Having the plates all on the end of the logs will make it easier to find them again when they are in a huge pile on the ground. You will be able to see the plates easily by walking around the outside of the pile, instead of having to move them around to get at a plate that is nailed on half way down the face of a log.

Before dismantling, lines parallel to the top wall plate are marked on the face of the lowest reusable log on each side of the building. If these logs are affixed on the new foundation with their lines level, the plates will turn out to be level also.

We have rebuilt several houses where the people who dismantled the building had not bothered to mark the logs or the marks had vanished. We managed to match up the logs by lining up paint marks, nail holes and window cuts — but the exercise is definitely *not* recommended.

There are various ways to number the logs. In the old days, when a building was dismantled to be moved, the logs were marked in roman numerals with an axe. Numbers marked in paint or felt tip pen are hard to read and may disappear altogether. After experimenting with various methods, we have found that the best one is using stainless steel or galvanized steel tags, about two inches square, with the numbers stamped on with a nail punch or stamp set. The best numbering system we have found is to mark the logs this way:

F for the front
B for the back
R for the right side
L for the left side.

Overleaf, left: The tree of life carved in this pine door, its roots formed in the wrought-iron of a massive hinge, makes an inviting entry.

Overleaf, right (clockwise): An imaginative north woods hideaway.
Stained glass is the focal point of this warm, inviting stairwell in the house shown at left.
This handmade light switch cover makes a worthy contribution to the constant struggle to conceal modern conveniences in an antique house.

Making a Diagram of Your Building

Another important step to take before you dismantle the logs is to make a diagram of the structure, taking note of all the relevant facts and measurements such as these:

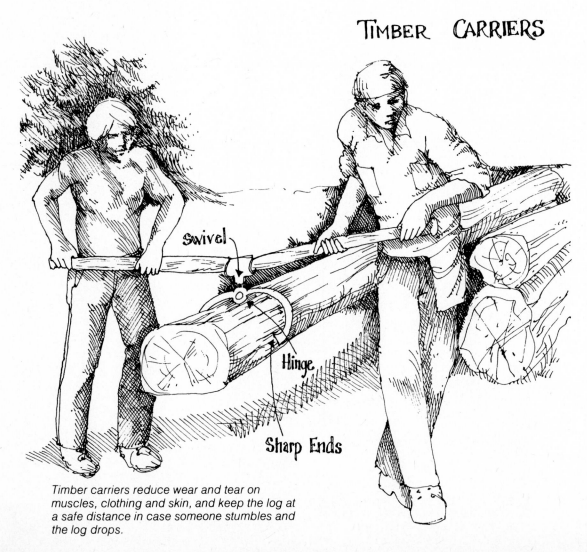

TIMBER CARRIERS

Swivel

Hinge

Sharp Ends

Timber carriers reduce wear and tear on muscles, clothing and skin, and keep the log at a safe distance in case someone stumbles and the log drops.

1. Location of all metal tags.

2. Precise outside dimensions of the building — measure each wall.

3. Overall height of the structure.

4. Any irregularities such as splices or blocks in the dovetails. (Number the blocks if you wish to reuse them.)

5. Location of existing stairwell.

6. Which of the bottom two logs to begin with when you begin reconstruction (i.e., front and back logs, or the left and right side logs).

7. Location and dimensions of logs to be replaced.

8. Distance from wall plate to top of second floor joists.

9. Distance from second floor joists to main floor.

10. Location and measurements of level lines. (See illustration of level line procedure on page 87.)

11. Location and size of windows and doors. (This will be invaluable in designing your new house.)

12. Dimensions of joists. *Note:* If joists are to be reused, mark them with metal tags or clusters of shiny, flat-headed nails, the number of nails corresponding to the number of the joist. Number them from left to right, facing the front of the building from the outside.

One more useful thing you could do before you dismantle the building is to take some photographs of the building from different angles. The photos can be used to check the original angle and lay of the logs in any moments of uncertainty during reconstruction.

Taking Your Log Building Apart

Almost without exception, the top two or three rounds of logs will be joined together with long wooden pegs or dowels. This is

THE CANT HOOK

The cant hook is a logger's tool that enables even a single person to handle large logs.

done to keep the rafters, which bear the weight of the roof and rest on the top (wall plate) log, from pushing the wall plate off the wall. So that these logs can be taken off one at a time and not stick together, these pegs must be removed, either by sticking a chain saw in between the logs and cutting them off or if you intend to reuse them, by prying them out with a crowbar. Make sure that there are no partition walls, window or door plates, or strapping holding the logs together — again so that the logs will come apart separately and smoothly. The short logs between the doors and windows (called filler logs) will fall down when unsupported by the buck plates and it is necessary to remove them by hand.

When you have made sure that the logs are free, you are ready to do the actual dismantling. It is important to be careful because even a big, stout-hearted log might break if dropped, and will have to be replaced. A dovetail broken in haste can take a long time to repair.

The easiest and safest method to dismantle the logs is to hire a long-bed logging truck with an articulated hydraulic claw (see photo on page 96) and a skilled operator. He will simply park the truck at a corner of the building and pick up the logs one at a time, setting them down on the flat bed truck. Carefully caution the operator on the need to go slowly and gently. Only two workers are needed for this operation — to free any logs that are stuck, and to straighten the load on the truck. Pile them straight and flat to prevent warping and breakage and to insure that they all will fit on one load.

That's the modern way to do it. The old-fashioned way uses manpower and gravity to slide the logs down two long poles called skids (see illustration on page 96). Any small tree will do for this; we usually use poplar because it's less brittle and has more spring than most trees. And with its reputation as the weed of the forest, we can cut it down with a clearer conscience. Peel the bark off these skids so that they are slippery. The length of the skids should be about twice the height of the walls of the building and their girth about five inches at the top. Put one end of each skid in the chink line under the top log (one skid about three feet in from each side) and anchor them securely in the ground. Then two men sit at the top of each end, roll the log onto the skids and lower it with ropes, while two people on the ground ease it down with poles or 2 x 4's. Use cant hooks or timber carriers (see tool section) to maneuver the logs over to the flat bed truck, then use the skids to load them on. Remember to save the skids if you are going to use this method to re-erect the logs.

When the logs arrive at the building site they should be stacked straight and flat so that they won't warp. Always put the pile up on a bed of old fence posts or something similar to keep them off the ground. Even a week's time on wet ground can cause the log faces to begin to pit and mold. If the logs are to sit for more than a month, scrap boards should be put between each layer of the pile to allow air to circulate between the logs and keep them dry.

A set of logs for a building should never be left in a pile outdoors for more than a year as water can readily run into the cracks, causing rot and frost splitting.

Note: Any discoloration caused by

Overleaf, left (clockwise): The design of this house shows the builder's great success with the difficult problem of combining old and modern materials and shapes. The house is built on a foundation which extends to just below the frost line, rather than forming a full basement. This was done to avoid having to remove or damage the trees which grow near the side of the house, and to keep the house low in its natural setting.

Windows such as these in the dining room cover the entire back of the house which forms a horseshoe shape around a garden carefully landscaped to retain the feeling of the surrounding forest.

The location of the fireplace creates an intimate seating spot between the dining room and the kitchen.

Overleaf, right: Bauhaus-style chrome chairs coexist splendidly with log walls and a nineteenth-century Polish-Canadian (Wilno) china hutch in this large bright room. The floor is made of 12-inch wide planks of cherrywood which the owner was fortunate to discover on a chance visit to a sawmill.

mildewing can be removed by brushing on a mixture of household chlorine bleach and water mixed 1:1. The logs can also be sandblasted if you want to remove the weathered appearance, but this should be done after the logs have been put back up because this is more convenient. When you are ready to begin reconstruction,

The old-fashioned way of raising or lowering logs (below) uses skids, poles and ropes. It's slow, but cheap— though you need friends to help. Opposite, you see a scaffold hoist, which is the method especially useful for high lifts, such as over a walkout basement.

Raising Logs by Hand

Push Pole

Poplar skid

Stake to hold skid.

carry the logs to their respective sides of the foundation and lay them out in the order that they will be erected. Be very careful with dovetail corners — they can break easily.

PUTTING IT BACK TOGETHER

Lifting Methods

SKIDS AND POLES
Using the skids and two men at the top pulling on ropes and four on the ground pushing with poles, simply reverse the dismantling procedure discussed on page 91. The only thing you might want to do differently is grease the skids so that the logs will slide up more easily. In the old days they used bacon fat for this.

SCAFFOLD HOIST
This is especially useful for high lifts such as over a walkout basement where skid poles would have to be an impossible length to reach the top log, or in places where trees or other obstructions make it impossible to use skids.

Rent three sections of standard five-foot steel scaffolding on coaster wheels and a half-ton block and tackle. Get twenty feet of steel I-beam and a half-ton trolley to run on the beam. Assemble this according to the illustration on page 95, and the photo on page 96. The logs may now be picked up from the outside of the wall, rolled back on the I-beam then lowered into place. This hoist can also be used to put the second floor joists into place and to lift roofing materials in bulk to the second floor. Care should be taken that the tower always be properly balanced and secured so it won't tip over. Place a plank under the wheels to spread the weight more evenly over the floor joists and prevent a wheel from breaking through the sub floor. The hoist must be on wheels so it can be rolled from wall to wall to make the lifts in the proper sequence. The bear paw or load binder in the counterbalance chain is used to make it easy to get the tension right again after the tower is moved.

HYDRAULIC CRANE
A hydraulic crane is big, fast and efficient (see photo on page 96). With it, a good-sized building can be put up in a day; however, the machine and its operator can be very expensive, especially when you consider that you have to pay for the travel time it takes for the crane to get to your site and for waiting time if there are any logs to be replaced or repaired as they go up. If you encounter any problems at all, this machine would likely be far too costly. Find out how much a crane in your area would actually cost, but if you foresee major problems, like replacing many logs, it might be best to resort to the following second and third lifting methods.

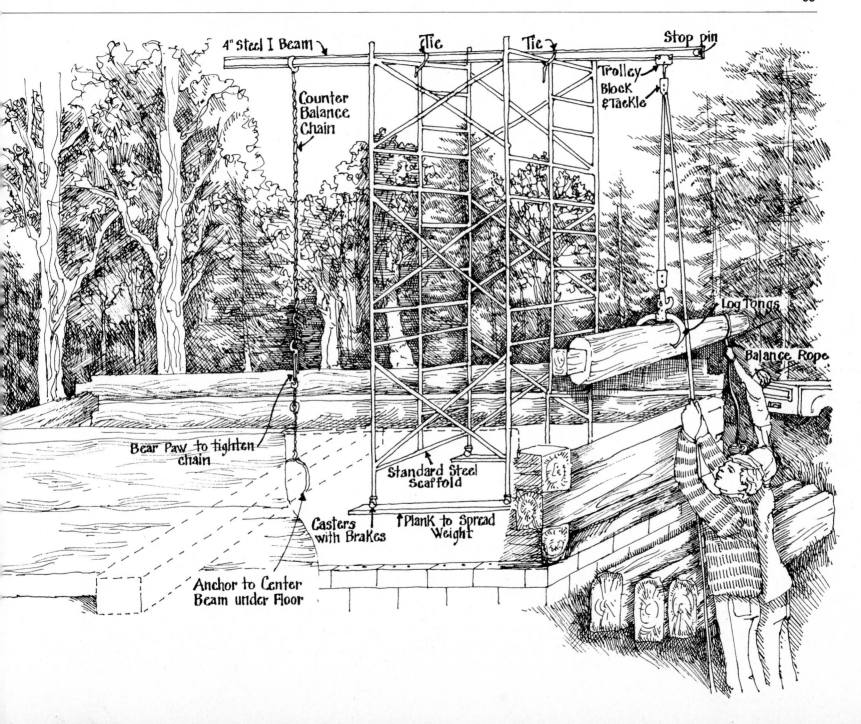

4" steel I Beam

Tie

Tie

Stop pin

Counter Balance Chain

Trolley Block & Tackle

Log Tongs

Balance Rope

Bear Paw to tighten chain

Standard Steel Scaffold

Casters with Brakes

↑Plank to Spread Weight

Anchor to Center Beam under Floor

Reconstructing The Log Walls

The level lines that were put on before the building was dismantled are marked on the lowermost log that is reusable. We will assume for the moment that the very bottom logs are in fact reusable.

Begin by putting in place the sill, or starter logs and putting on both end logs so that you have one complete round down. Now adjust the height of these logs until the lines which you put on before dismantling all come level, or in other words are parallel with the foundation, and block them in place. The builder will then be easily able to see at what point the sill logs may be cut to provide a good flat bottom to sit on the foundation without cutting off more than is necessary. These level lines which you have marked on the building are actually parallel to the top wall plates. If they are made to be parallel to the foundation when they are put in place, it follows that the wall plates must also be parallel to the foundation when they are reached. If the foundation is level, then the wall plates will have to be level as well.

If the lowermost original logs have rotted away, then you will have placed the level lines on the next course up. If this is the case, you will have to put these logs down in place first and block them up until the lines come parallel to the foundation. Block up high enough so that the logs which will replace the original bottom logs can fit underneath. By taking measurements between the foundation and the course of level logs, you can determine the exact size and shape of the replace-

Above, a hydraulic crane erecting logs for the barn on page 85. Below, one man and several hundred horses dismantle a barn.

foundation with stone or brick, you can skip this step and simply bring the stone right up to the bottom of the side log.)

Putting the log walls up is certainly the most satisfying part of reconstructing an old building. The danger here, however, is that you will become so impatient to see the walls finished and up that you will work too fast. It is important to work slowly and carefully, and to make sure that the corners are going up straight and level — by *checking after every round* of logs has been put up. (If you wait until later to make corrections, the sheer weight of the logs will make it very difficult.) You can check this by taping a spirit level to a straight edge board and placing it against the corners of the building. If any adjustments

Logs being sorted, checked and repaired in preparation for reconstruction.

ment logs which are to go underneath.

While you have the starter course blocked in place, and before you make any cuts, you should take this final opportunity to make sure that the first floor ceiling height will be adequate when it is reached. If you have to cut too much off the sill logs to get them to sit flat and right the first floor ceiling may be too low, especially since many older buildings have low ceilings to begin with. If this is the case, you may find it easiest to put the necessary new course of logs underneath the original first round. If this is done, then the level lines may still be used as before. If the extra logs are added later, they can

put the building out of level. When deciding what to do, you must take into account the final height of the tops of the first floor doors and windows.

Another problem to be dealt with is the gap between the bottom of the end logs, which sit on the starter logs, and the foundation. This gap is usually too big to chink. A good solution is to cut a log the right height to fit into this gap, with the flat cut edge sitting on the foundation and the rounded edge coming up to within about two inches of the bottom of the end log. (See illustration on page 61.) This gives you a small enough chink line to work with, and it can look very attractive with the flat side of the cut log seeming to disappear into the foundation. (If you are using a stone foundation, or facing a cement

Overleaf, left: The master bedroom of the house shown on pages 106 and 107, looking through the front dormer of the house.

The section on the right is the original, century-old farmstead on this property. The owner brought us in to build the frame entrance foyer and the Georgian-style wing on the left. At the same time, we had to do extensive reworking of the original wing to correct problems caused by renovations five years earlier. The chinking had been put in wrong, causing the logs to remain wet and water to run inside. The roof and cellar had not been vented, causing dry rot in the main beams, mildewing odors, and curling shingles.

Overleaf, right: This log guest house, on the same property as the modern log house shown on pages 92 and 93, stays much closer to traditional materials and shapes than does the main house. The interior is furnished completely with antiques.

This system is used so that replacement logs can be made up in advance and be ready to go when the hydraulic crane or building crew arrives to put them up. It saves stopping the whole show each time a replacement must be cut in.

If time is no problem, the system used for cutting new dovetails will also work.

Lay the old log to be replaced (right hand in sketch) up on skids so that its face is plumb, as it would be in place in the wall. Set the replacement log up beside it in the same manner, with its face also plumb. Using a level, transfer the high points of the dovetail onto the butt end of the new log. Using a bevel gauge and level as shown, determine the angles of the old dovetail and transfer them to the new log end at the points previously marked. A level is used rather than pressing the handle of the bevel gauge against the face of the log because the log face is usually too rough and irregular for good accuracy. Transfer the side angles of the dovetail in the same manner, and cut it out as shown in dovetail sequence.

Duplicating a Dovetail for Replacement

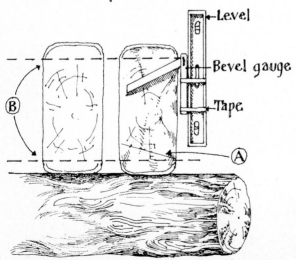

Level

Bevel gauge

Tape

B

A

are required, the stray log can be drifted into place with a heavy wooden sledge hammer. If you use a steel sledge hammer, hold a piece of wood between the hammer and the log so you don't bruise the log.

Sometimes you will find you still have to make adjustments to a log after other logs have been added on top of it. To accomplish this, take a steel bar about six feet long, stick it between the logs of the wall adjacent to the problem log, and with the proper leverage you can lift five or six logs off a corner where you need to do any additional work.

As you begin putting up the short logs which run between the corners and the window openings, you will have to put blocks under the butt ends to a height that will allow their dovetails to sit properly closed. You may also find it necessary to brace up these small corner logs until the continuous log which goes above the window and door openings can be put in place. The small filler logs that have no dovetails (because they run between two openings in the same wall) are put in after the whole building is up, as we explain later.

Some houses were originally built with the corners tapering in slightly toward the top, rather than being plumb and level (exactly vertical), although it isn't known just why this was done. If your building had such a taper and you have not noticed it in your pre-dismantling diagram, trying to make it plumb as it goes up will likely be a pretty frustrating job. In other words, if the top log is two inches shorter than the bottom log, as it might easily be, the corners can't possibly come out perfectly vertical, and the walls will slope inward. If such a problem is spotted from the very beginning, some careful cutting,

measuring and adjusting — beginning with the bottom round of logs — can set the walls straight.

Any sloping of the original walls is best detected by measuring the length of any particular wall face at the bottom, middle and top. If the logs decrease in length, the wall will slope inward. If the logs increase in length as you go up, they will slope outward. Any outward slope should definitely be avoided. The offending logs will have to be shortened by cutting the dovetails deeper.

Unless the difference is severe, the end result will be barely visible and most people would have no trouble living with slightly inward sloping walls.

In any wall which has a door in it, you can easily correct sloping walls by setting the bottom log (which will be two pieces separated by an opening), the same length as the first continuous log over the door. Such a change should be noticed and planned for before the foundation is built.

Tape measures were not in common use when old log houses were built, so the length of logs in one building may vary quite a bit from top to bottom and from side to side. Never assume that any two logs are of the same length.

Properly notched and fitted dovetail corners are the hallmark of a well-reconstructed log building.

Second Floor Joists

When you reach the log that carries the second floor joists, you will be able to determine the line followed by the original second floor. Measure from this line down to the first floor, all the way along the length of the building. These measurements will tell you if you have reached the second floor stage with everything level. If you haven't, you can then take steps to

Tower lift stands ready to hoist the logs of a century-old frontier hotel onto the walls at their new location. Note the metal marking tags on corners; temporary support blocks between the ends of the short logs; two-inch planks nailed on to reinforce logs where they are cut for windows during the move; the upright beam in the center of the house which is the main beam for an eventual spiral staircase.

The butt ends of these second floor planks disappear neatly into slots cut in the logs. This is by far the best way to support the planks around the perimeter of the house.

correct it. If, for instance, one corner is dipping an inch lower than the other, the high side can be lowered by taking off an inch of wood from the dovetails on that side, a little from each notch. Of course instead of this, you could put a one-inch block in the dovetail joint on the low side, but this block would be visible in the notch and ruin the continuity of the interlocking corners. Blocks should only be used as a last resort, as in a case where the error

you are trying to correct is so great that you can't cut out the required amount from the dovetails without the logs touching. This corrective work can also be done to the last four or five rounds of logs that are now placed on top of the joist carrier logs, right up to the last ones (the wall plates), which are the uppermost logs running the length of the building. The floor joists can then be brought level by placing shims under their ends.

If you are using a scaffold hoist, you won't be able to put in the second floor joists until all the logs are up. In this case, logs above the joist carrier logs can be pushed outward to allow the joists to be dropped into their pockets, then pushed back into place.

Wall Plates

Most logs in a building are hewn only on two sides (inside and outside). The wall

plates, however, are squared on three sides to provide a flat surface to sit the rafters on. If you follow the leveling procedure described earlier, you should arrive at the top with a flat, level surface from which roof framing may be started. Notches will have been cut into the top outside surface of the wall plates to accept the round rafters in the original building. Water damage, removal of spikes, and the probability that new rafters will have to be spaced differently to accommodate insulation and 4 x 8 plywood sheeting, etc., will render these wall plates unsuitable for mounting the roof rafters.

After you are sure the wall plates are

level, a 2- x 6-inch board can be placed on top of both plates. These are called "nailers," and they give you something smooth and perfectly level to set the rafters on. Take care to insure that the nailers are parallel, even if it means overhanging or underhanging them a little bit on the wall plates. If the overhang is going to be more than an inch, strengthen the nailers by doubling them. If the nailers are not parallel, your rafters will get further and further apart, and the roof will be crooked.

Before spiking the nailers in all the way, put wooden shims under any low spots so they will be free of dips or humps. Shims are lower quality cedar shingles that taper from about half an inch to a point, and you can buy them cheaply by the bale. These pieces of tapered cedar can be driven under the 2 x 6 narrow end first, until it has lifted the piece to whatever height is desired. The protruding piece can then be broken off with a hammer so that it is flush with the log or 2 x 6.

Pegging

As we have mentioned before, the top two or three logs are pegged together about three feet in from each corner, so that the roof rafters won't push the top log off the wall. If you can, use the original pegs that you removed during dismantling (these were often made of ironwood or hop hornbeam, which was also used for sleigh runners and axe handles). Sometimes you can't recycle the pegs because you have cut them off with a chain saw when you couldn't pry them out, or maybe the holes have shifted, leaving you no choice but to drill new ones. This is one of the few areas where even purists can be tempted to veer away from the traditional. We use a one-inch steel bar, about three feet long.

Holes for wooden pegs need to be quite large but steel pegs give the same strength, with smaller holes, thus allowing either the use of power tools, or an easier job with hand tools. So that we could drill a three-foot hole, we had a metal shop weld a one-inch auger bit onto a long steel shaft. The old-style auger bits are the best because they have a longer spiral twist (auger) to take away the chips. The longer this twist is, the less chance there is of the bit getting jammed up with wood chips and stuck in the peg-hole. In any case, when you are drilling these holes, pull the drill out every two inches or so to remove the wood chips. Note that flat speed bores jam constantly and should be avoided.

After the wall plates have been pegged, there is one more thing you could do to them to keep a long roof from sagging later on. Drive a wedge or shim in under the middle of the plate, so that it bows up slightly to compensate for any slight settling that might occur in future.

An important note of caution: "Gone south" is an expression carpenters use to describe what happens to hammers or other tools that fall off a joist or high log and land in the basement. People can also go south. If the drill jams suddenly and twists, it can throw you right off the wall, so make sure you tie yourself on to something securely with a rope.

Windows and Doors

Keep in mind that none of the short filler logs are put in until all the long logs are up. The filler logs are the short pieces that go in between the windows and doors, the ones that don't have any dovetails. Any changes done to the windows and doors from the original building will have to be planned ahead so that when you are ready to put in the filler logs, you will know

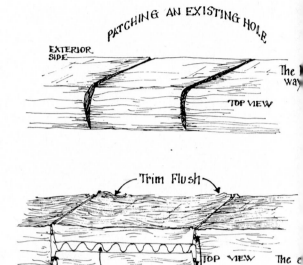

Patching up an unwanted hole in a log wall. The cumbersome and irregular nature of the logs makes it impossible to cut a plug so accurately that all four visible joint lines will be tight and will remain closed. It will simplify the task if the plug is cut in half and about an inch of wood is removed from the back of each half. The inside and outside face can then be dealt with separately. The plug piece is cut just slightly larger than the opening and the edges are cut on a slight angle or wedge shape. Caulking is put along the joint and the piece is driven into place. Any part of the plug which protrudes beyond the face of the log is then trimmed off with a chisel or adze. The plug should be close enough to the actual size of the opening that no more than 1/4 inch need be trimmed off. The plug will finally be nailed in place.

Pegs should be driven through the logs to either side of the patch to secure them against lateral movement.

This type of patching must obviously take place after the logs are in place in the wall.

Two methods of joining interior partitions or buildings together. These are two barns at Black Creek Pioneer Village.

and windows is to make them larger than their actual size by half an inch on either side, and an inch or more on the top. These gaps will be covered up by the trim you'll put on later.

Wait until the roof and interior framing have been done before you install the windows and doors. This period will give the building a chance to settle into place, and will also prevent doors and windows from being damaged while rough work is going on. This is a good time to order the window and door units so they will be ready when you need them.

BUCK PLATES
You will also have to allow for the thickness of the rough buck plates on either side. (See illustration of double-hung windows on page 42.)

exactly where to notch your frames and how long to cut the filler logs.

As you probably know, all buildings shift with time and temperature changes. This is especially true of log buildings, since wood is a living organic material that expands when it's hot and humid and contracts when it's cold and dry. Don't forget to take this into consideration when you are reconstructing a house, especially when allowing for the placement of windows and doors. If they sit too tight in the walls, the change of dimensions due to humidity change can squash the frame and the window glass will crack or the door will stick. A good rule of thumb to use when cutting out rough openings for doors

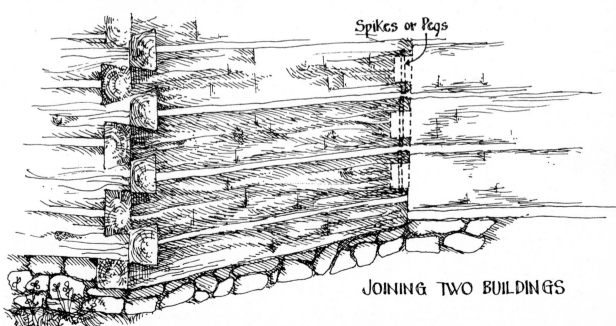

Spikes or Pegs

JOINING TWO BUILDINGS

This method is not at all the same when using green logs. When building a new log house, you make the top clearance considerably larger and a sliding channel buck plate is used. (For full explanation see the "Long Log" section in Chapter 4.)

The width of the buck plates should be two inches narrower than the thickness of the logs: 2- x 6-inch spruce will suffice for eight-inch logs. They are notched into the logs above and below the opening. The filler logs are fastened to the buck plates with six-inch spikes.

Before doing the actual cutting, lay out all the openings on the wall with a pencil and chalk line, and double check every measurement. Then cut the ends of the logs off along this line with a chain saw. This is for increasing the width of the window openings. If you want to increase the height of the opening, make chain saw cuts to the line every six inches, then pop the sections out with a crowbar and finish with an axe (see illustration). Notch the buck plates about one inch into the top and bottom logs; if the filler logs are extremely large and heavy, double the number of buck plates.

When the plates are in and you have cut the filler logs to the correct length, you can fit them into the wall. When doing this, keep in mind that these logs were originally part of a continuous tree and that the windows and doors were cut out after the solid walls were put up. You should try to maintain this continuity by standing back and lining up the short logs with the ones on either side of the opening. When lining up the vertical faces on the interior and exterior, keep in mind that on the exterior you would like to have as flat a surface as possible so you can seal the gap around the eventual trim. Secure the filler logs in place with small nails that can be pulled easily until the whole section you are working on is spaced and situated correctly, then drive two six-inch spikes into each log end to make them permanent.

Cutting Out for Openings

③ Finish with axe
② Break cut chunks
① Cut to line
Cut out line

LOCATION OF SASH IN FRAME
In thick-wall construction, the window sash should be set in the frame so that it is toward the outside wall surface, leaving the most depth to the inside to form large and convenient window sills. When using aluminum storms, leave enough space between the main sash and the storm so that when the storms are slid apart to be repaired or cleaned the bottom storms

Some log faces which protrude farther than others have been cut into so the trim will sit flat on the wall, eliminating ugly gaps and making the unit more windproof. The rear of the exterior chinking is seen in the gaps between the logs. The interior will be completely trimmed after the foam is sprayed in but before the interior chinking mortar is applied so that it will come tight against the trim and form a seal.

which come off first won't get jammed between the upper storm, the check rail in the middle and the window sill, in which case you would not be able to get either the window or the screen out.

When working with old well-seasoned

DETAIL OF WOODEN WATER SHED CAP

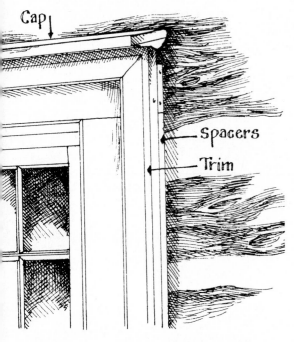

Cap

Spacers

Trim

BLOCKING

Now that the log work is complete, go over the entire building and put blocks between all the rounds of logs to keep them from sagging. These blocks should be inserted at least every six feet, and should be narrow enough that they do not interfere with the space to be taken up by the chinking.

SANDBLASTING

The interiors of old log buildings have frequently been whitewashed, painted, plastered or otherwise discolored. The quickest and most effective method of restoring the color of the wood is to sandblast. We usually have our buildings

Overleaf, left: This house was designed to appear as a simple traditional log house from the front, its true size showing only at the back. The windows, custom-made for us by a local wood shop, are covered by brown aluminum storms, which are all but invisible.

Overleaf, right (clockwise): U-shaped kitchens such as this are very practical and efficient to work in. Kitchen activity is kept out of the eating and sitting area, but the person doing the work is not isolated from the general gathering of people.

Two photos from different angles in the living room of the same house. The railing, banisters and the newel posts of the stairs are from the original house, but the staircase itself was made especially to suit the new height of the building. The pine plank floors are new wood with an antiquing stain. The original building measured twenty-four feet by thirty-four feet, unusually large for a log house.

The interior of one of the porch wings at the rear of the house.

When building with logs which are not perfectly seasoned and dry, the trim cannot be recessed into the wall to prevent water from running in behind it, because any settling of the logs during drying will crush the trim. In such cases a wooden drip cap is nailed on to cover any gap behind the trim and caulking is put on to complete the seal. Any gap between the vertical trim boards is filled with a spacer and caulked. Trim is nailed to the window unit only, not to the logs.

This pine window casing has been cut into the logs so that the face of the top part is flush with the face of the log. The small metal drip cap and silicone caulking provide further assurance that water will never find its way behind the trim and rot the window unit. Note that this recessed application is only possible with well-seasoned logs as a green log wall would shrink in height and crush the trim.

logs, the window frame should be located in the opening so that when trim is nailed on, its face will be flush with the exterior face of the building. This will prevent water

from running behind and rotting the frame. In new log construction, the logs will shrink so much that they would destroy trim installed in a recessed fashion.

CHINKING DETAIL
CROSS SECTION VIEW

INTERIOR

Vapor barrier
(not needed with
foam)

Plaster

Wire mesh

1" Galvanized
roofing nail-
large head

LOG

EXTERIOR

Chinking recessed
to shed water

Insulation

Plaster

Wire mesh

Log

This photo shows the blocking put between the logs to keep them from sagging along their length as explained on page 104. Also seen is the 1/2-inch mesh galvanized chicken wire which will form the base for the chinking mortar. It is recessed far enough that the wire will not show through the final mortar coat.

The two Xs carved in the face of the log in the lower right portion of the photo are roman numerals used to code the logs when they were moved at some time in the past. We discovered that some old buildings had made several moves around the countryside to fill the changing needs of settlement and growth.

sandblasted both inside and out to give them a uniform appearance and a color which will more closely match the new wood used in their reconstruction. For the sake of both convenience and uniformity this is done after all the log and timber work is in place.

A very light touch by a professional is necessary when sandblasting so as not to erase the hewing marks and other details

which give the logs character. The blaster will readily remove the soft wood between the hard layers in the grain creating a pitted appearance similar to driftwood if the spray is directed in one place too long. Also, any hard spots such as paint or plaster should be scraped or broken off before blasting because the blaster would have to dwell longer on the hard spots and therefore cut too heavily into adjacent areas of exposed wood. Always do a test on a piece of discarded log to get the feel of things before starting on the house itself.

CHINKING

One of the last steps in constructing the traditional hewn log house is filling and sealing the gaps between the logs. This is called "chinking." There is some discussion as to whether the term chinking refers to the whole process or only to the material

used to plug up the gaps. Here we will refer to the process and to the material used as "chinking," and to the gaps themselves as "chinks."

You will do the chinking after all the windows and doors are in place and trimmed and the electrical wiring has been installed. The openings must be trimmed first so that the chinking can be brought up tightly against the trim, forming a good seal against the weather.

In the early days of log building, the builders filled the chinks by hammering in pieces of split cedar rail, or in some cases stones, which provided a base for a sealing coat of lime plaster, clay, moss, moss with lime or whatever was on hand. For those of you who are purists or just inclined to use whatever you find lying around, we'll tell you that we once found a set of barns in Quebec that were chinked with manure and straw, and the owner told us that he had no complaints about this method.

These old methods have proved inadequate because they leave a rather large area of the wall, which is comprised of chinking, uninsulated. There is also no secondary barrier to keep out wind where the chinking cracks, as it always does with time.

Here is the modern five-step method for chinking:

1. Apply wire lath along the exterior of the chink. (Lath is any material used to support plaster.)
2. Put on the outside chinking.
3. Put in insulation, and, if necessary, a vapor barrier.
4. Apply wire lath along the inside of the chink.
5. Apply inside chinking.

Lath

You could use red wire plasterer's lath of the type which is used in regular plaster walls. The problem with this material is that red stains might appear on the chinking caused by the wire rusting inside. It is also very stiff to work into irregular-shaped gaps, and the cut edges are very sharp. However, its extra strength makes it good for areas larger than four inches.

We have been told that fine wire cloth, which is available from some building supply stores, is very pliable, and easy to cut and work with.

We ourselves have found that half-inch galvanizing chicken wire mesh serves very

Careful attention should be paid to keeping the size of chinks to a minimum to avoid wide mortar courses such as the one over the porch of this otherwise well-conceived house.

well. The galvanizing process prevents the appearance of rust stains on the chinking later and the wire is easy to work, while still providing good strength to reinforce the mortar. It is widely available at hardware stores and farm suppliers. It comes in wide rolls which are cut into sections wide enough to cover the chink when the mesh is unrolled. The wire mesh can be stretched to cover large holes or folded to fit small ones. The large rolls can be cut with a hacksaw or, believe it or not, with a circular saw. Make sure you use an old blade, and wear goggles for this part. Don't cut up the whole roll until you have experimented a bit to find which widths suit your house best.

Lath must be put everywhere the chinking is to go, including gaps around window and door trim. When putting it in the chinks themselves, there is a tendency to put it too close to the face of the log because it is hard to reach in further with a hammer to drive the nails. Be careful to see that the lath is fastened back far enough that it won't show through the chinking.

Mortar

The mortar used for chinking should tend to be a bit soft, to reduce cracking as the logs expand and contract during humidity changes. Regular cement or mortar mix is a bit too hard. Also it is gray, whereas most people prefer a white chinking.

To make the mortar soft, you must add lime to the mix (see mortar table in appendix). Lime also has the desirable effect of making the mortar more plastic, therefore easier to apply, whiter, and giving it better sticking ability.

The mortar sand should be fine, sharp brick-sand, free of rocks and bits of organic material. The water should be clean enough to be almost drinkable. Don't use swamp water.

Always mix the aggregate (cement, sand, etc.) first and then add the water. When you add the water to the mix, it seems to have very little effect at first, but toward the end, you discover that a little goes a long way — the mix can become soupy very quickly. It is not a good idea to add more cement to thicken it up, so add the water a little at a time until you get the feel of it. Do not add more water if the mortar begins to harden as you are using it. If it hardens too much to use, throw it out. Mix it up in small batches, and keep it out of the sun. The mortar is the right consistency when you take some on a trowel, and turn it over slowly without any falling off until the trowel is four-fifths of the way to being vertical.

The chinking should be put on in two coats, unless the chink is quite small, because the first coat tends to slump or slide out before it can set. Scratch the first coat with the tip of the trowel so the second coat will have something to "key" or bond to. Also, to promote bonding, the first coat should still be damp when the second coat is applied. If it has dried out by the time you come back to it, just sprinkle on some more water.

FREEZING

If the mortar freezes before it can dry, it will not cure properly, and the result will be flaky and crumbly. In moderate freezing weather (26 degrees Fahrenheit), some calcium can be added to the mix, which produces heat through chemical reaction sufficient to last while the mortar is setting. Too much calcium will weaken the mix. (See the instructions on the calcium bag.)

MOISTURE

If the logs are bone dry, they may draw the moisture out of the mortar before it has a chance to cure. If you notice that the mortar is drying much faster around the edges than in the center, dampen the logs slightly. If the logs are soggy after a heavy rain, they will have swollen up. If you put the chinking in while they are soaking wet, the logs will shrink when the sun comes out and cracks will open up around the chinking. Very hot, direct sun will also dry the mortar too fast.

Insulation

There is much discussion as to which kind of insulation is the best. Until some precise scientific testing is done, no one can say with any certainty whether urethane foam or fiberglass batts are better.

From our experience, we have found that urethane foam does the best job. It has a much greater insulation factor than fiberglass which is a great advantage considering the limited space between the courses of chinking. It forms a weather-tight seal as it bonds strongly to the wood, and is itself windproof. Movement of the logs is bound to crack the chinking in a number of places allowing the wind in. This is one of the reasons why many early log cabin builders were pleased when they could finally afford wood board siding for their drafty dwellings. The foam seals excellently around doors, windows and dovetails, those areas which are impossible to chink properly because they are so narrow.

If you pack fiberglass in hard enough to stop the wind it loses all its insulative qualities as there are no air pockets left in it. If it is put in fully expanded, the wind will go right through it. Also, any water which gets around the chinking will sit in the fiberglass, ruining its insulation properties and rotting the logs. Fiberglass takes more time to put in, and requires the extra step of putting in a vapor barrier which urethane does not need. One thing to highly recommend fiberglass is that it is much cheaper.

One interesting chinking method that we heard of from Oklahoma State University consists of painting the inside of the chink with spar varnish. Let it get a little tacky, and then put in some rock wool (glass wool) and bang it into place inside the chink. Now coat the rock wool with linseed oil for an elastic, weather-resistant chinking. We have never actually seen this method used ourselves, but our sources at Oklahoma State tell us that it works well for them.

Chinking is one of the many skills that looks easy when you watch the pros doing it, but proves a little more difficult when you pick up the trowel to try it yourself. We have seen a crew of two professional chinkers and one helper do an 18 x 24 house with 12-foot high walls, inside and out (including wire lath) in less than two days. We tried it ourselves once on the same size building, and it took us a week — and then some. There is a certain trick of the wrist you need to master when using a trowel, and a feeling for mixing mortar that takes a while to acquire. Speed also depends on the size of the chinks and the amount of scaffolding that must be rigged to reach them.

With the chinking taken care of, the shell of the house is completed. The work remaining to finish the house relies less on muscle power and more on your own creativity and taste.

Cutting a Dovetail

In the following series of photos Len Van Dyk shows us how to cut a dovetail joint. We chose to demonstrate the simple dovetail rather than the compound angle type shown in the first chapter, because the simple type is less confusing than the compound and does the job just as well. The application of the same techniques shown here, plus a little logic will enable a clever builder to cut the compound type although in our opinion the extra angles do not improve the strength of the corners. Instead they are weakened by increasing the number of sharp points which are prone to splitting and breaking.

The method used here allows both the first and second log, that is, both the front and side log, to sit flat on the foundation rather than having a large gap under the second log to deal with as discussed on page 61 in this chapter.

Note that the tree bark should always be removed from the top and bottom of the logs before use. If left on, it acts as a sponge holding water in the chink line and also makes a very unstable surface to apply the chinking to. In the past it was a common practice to char the tops and bottoms of building logs in a fire to cauterize the wood cells, thereby preventing decay. Considering the fine chemical preservatives available today, charring should not be necessary.

A step which is not shown here is cutting the logs to length. Rough cut each log about 6 inches longer than necessary so it can be cut to final length in position on the wall after the log has been blocked up to its final angle of lay and before the corner joint is marked. A level is used to mark the end cuts, ensuring that the butt of the log will be in a vertical plane regardless of the lay of the log.

1. *The first log worked on is the one which will be the second log up. This log is flattened on the bottom so it will sit flat and square on the foundation. The second log is worked on first so that its exact width (height) will be known and can be used in figuring the exact size and shape of the log below it which will be cut next. This reversal of working order only occurs with the first round of logs.*

From your stock of logs pick one of the largest and straightest ones. If it has any curve at all make the bowed or convex edge the top. Using your chalk line, mark a line on the bottom of the logs face in a spot which will allow you to cut the least amount off the log and still attain a straight flat surface. This line should be parallel to the top of the log.

2. You could cut along the line which you have just marked on with a chain saw or you could score up to the line with a chain saw and hew off the wood with an adze as Len has chosen to do here. Either method will work well, but if your chain saw is less than perfectly sharp or is small and lacks the necessary power, hewing will be your quickest and most accurate choice. When hewing, mark the cut line on both faces and the butt ends of the log to insure accuracy.

3. Break out the blocks between the score cuts with an adze then go back over the surface and smooth it out. Never cut your marking line completely off when hewing. Steel-toed boots and sober judgement are recommended when using the adze.

4. *Measure the final width (height) of the log which you have cut in the first three steps, then chalk line and cut another log to be half of that width. This log will actually be the first one down, its sawn edge sitting on the foundation.*

This log is cut so that its crown (top) is parallel to its base. Cut the ends square and clean.

Note the chips from the saw are long and string-like rather than granular, indicating a sharp saw. A dull saw will tend to run off the cut line if the teeth on one side of the chain are sharper than those on the other side.

5. *Set your bevel gauge to about 75 degrees (angle marked X on log end in photo). Hold the handle against the inside face of the log and put on a line, fairly close to the top of the log, in order to leave enough wood to give the dovetail strength. This angle is always made so that it will slope downward and outward toward the exterior of the wall.*

7. Draw horizontal lines from both ends of the bevel line back along the faces of the log. Now draw a perpendicular line down from the shoulder line which was previously marked across the top of the log, to intersect with the horizontal line.

6. Mark a line across the top of the log which is located by measuring in from the butt end a distance equal to the thickness of the log which will go on top; in this case the log which was dealt with in the first three photos. This line is made at right angles to the face of the log. It marks out what is called the shoulder of the log.

8. Now cut carefully down to the line in three places as shown in the photo. Don't cut right to the line, but leave 1/8 inch or more of wood above the line.

SOCKET
SLICK

9. *Cut out the blocks between the saw cuts as shown.*

10. *With mallet and chisel, carefully cut the wood away right up to the line all around the edge of the joint.*

11. With a socket slick or regular chisel cut down the wood in the center of the joint until it is flush with the chiseled surface (which you have made in the previous step) around the edge of the joint.

If the face of the joint you are working on will face upward when it is in place in the wall, cut the center of the joint face flush with the outside edges. The downward-facing joint which will sit on top should be dished out slightly to prevent any high spots in the center of the face from holding the joint open around the edges. The upward-facing joint surfaces are not dished out in this manner to prevent water from collecting there, should any seep in past the edges of the joint.

12. Place the logs in the exact position on the foundation where they will eventually rest. Don't forget that the logs should always overhang the foundation by 1/2 inch, to shed any water which may run down the walls, and that their tops should be level.

Measure the gap between the bottom of the second log and the foundation. In this case we have five inches.

13. *Apply the distance determined in the previous step to the shoulder line of the second log and make a mark. Mark on the perpendicular shoulder line as shown.*

14. *Apply the same measurement to the butt end of the log at both sides of the butt. Connect these marks and continue the line across the face of the log to connect with the shoulder line. Do the same on the inside face of the log as well. What we have done here is to make a series of lines around the end of the second log which are parallel to the edges of the joint face of the first log.*

15. *Roll the log over and cut out the joint which you have marked in the previous two steps in the same manner as the joint on the first log was cut out. Note that the cut for this joint will be made on a diagonal line to the grain, and extra care must be taken to prevent splits from occurring. Always drive your chisel down the slope of the joint. If you drive it up the slope, it will catch under the grain and break the joint. If you do split off a piece of the joint, it can generally be nailed back into place.*

Roll the log back into place; if you have made your measurements properly, the bottom of the second log should sit down flat on the foundation and the joint should be perfectly closed.

When the whole first course of logs is complete, they can be anchored to the foundation in one of the ways described in the Long Log section of Chapter 4.

16. *Using the bevel gauge mark on cut lines in the same manner as described for log number one on the top of the second log. Once again the slope of the joint should be downward and outward. Cut out the joint as before.*

17. *Lay the third log in place and transfer the contours or shape of the joint on the top of the second log onto the bottom of the third log. The height at which these lines are marked is determined by measuring the distance between the bottom of the third log and the top of the first log in the space where the chinking will go. Take this measurement and subtract between two to two-and-a-half inches which will be the two inches or so left between the logs*

for chinking. You will have to vary the size of the chink space occasionally in the interest of getting the wall to come out level at the top, keeping in mind that too small a gap is difficult to chink and too large a gap is unsightly. With the exception of the first round and the last, the tops of each round of logs will not be level but rather their location will depend on the size of the logs which will follow. On each course of logs, the taper will be the reverse of the last course, except in situations where you may need to put two big ends consecutively in order to bring up a low corner. All subsequent dovetails are cut in the same manner as the one described in the last step.

As you get higher up on the wall you will find it necessary to put a plank diagonally across

the corner of the house so you can perch on it while working. Both ends of the log are worked on simultaneously; that is both ends must be marked before either is cut, otherwise the log will not be at the correct horizontal angle for marking and the angles of the second joint will be wrong. For this reason, it is convenient to have two corner people working on each end of the same log, hence saving a lot of climbing back and forth.

As a final refinement, the top of the exterior face of each dovetail can be trimmed off about 1/8 inch with a socket slick so that the butt end of the joint above it will overhang the face slightly. This provides a sharp drip ledge which will cause water to drop off rather than run into the joint by capillary action.

18. *The finished dovetail notches.*

building with round logs

Whatever style of building you decide upon, the first question to be answered is where to get your logs. There are several alternatives:

1. Cutting your own out of the bush.
2. Buying them from a logger, a farmer, a log builder or government.
3. Using old barn logs.

Cutting Your Own

Essentially, this means you will be doing your own logging, and will entail much more work than you might think. However, it allows you to pick your own trees, getting exactly the size and species you want. Take your time when selecting which trees to cut. Walk all around the tree, look at it from underneath, from a distance, from different angles. Look for trees that will give you straight logs of the length and diameter that you will need.

Softwoods are the species recommended for log building. When a tree has been felled and dried, the tiny cells that make up the wood seal up into separate, airtight compartments, forming air pockets which provide good insulation. Softwoods are less dense than hardwoods, and the walls of the cells are thinner; consequently the wood is softer and easier to work with. The most common species used for log houses are red and white pine (most favored by Eastern log builders), western red and eastern white cedar, balsam, spruce, fir, poplar and hemlock. The more smooth and regular the trees are, the easier they are to build with.

There is some disagreement among log builders about exactly when is the best time to cut the trees down and remove the bark. Some people say it's winter, while others swear by the spring. Trees cut in the spring have the sap still running in them, which forms a layer of moisture between the bark and the sapwood. This makes it easier to peel the bark off instead of having to use a drawknife to scrape it off. This labor-saving way of removing the bark is the one distinct advantage of cutting in the spring, other than the fact that sap-peeled logs have a smooth, unmarked lustre to them which drawknifed logs don't have.

To sap-peel logs, use a flat-nosed garden spade and run the blade along the log, splitting the bark and then peeling it off. This process goes very quickly — a large poplar that has been well limbed takes about ten minutes to peel. It's a sticky messy business, so wear old clothes and wash the sap off immediately with a petroleum solvent. Logs cut in the spring should be stacked in the shade so they will dry slowly and not "check." Cover them with a tarpaulin if there is no shady spot nearby.

A tree that is cut in the winter has none of the sugary sap rising up from the roots because it's dormant. The logs cut from winter trees have less water content that must be air-dried out, and therefore there is less chance of checking as they are dried. Checking is caused by uneven drying — the heart of the tree dries more slowly than the outside, creating a tension which splits the wood. The fact that there is no sap also means less moisture for the growth of the fungus that causes

mildewing and sap stain. We have always preferred to log in the winter, logging being one of the few things that the snow makes easier. Horses like to haul in the snow and, best of all, there are no bugs in the winter bush. Actually the only disadvantage to cutting in the winter is that you can't sap-peel the logs and must drawknife the bark off them. This results in a tiger-stripe effect on the logs which some people like and others don't.

Whether you like the effect or not, drawknifing takes time and is a lot of hard work. To make it easier it is important to use the right kind of drawknife. The kind usually available in hardware stores has a straight blade that keeps the two handles low, causing your knuckles to scrape and bang against the log, especially if it is a wide log. It also has a chisel-like bevel that tends to dig into the log as you pull. This particular kind of drawknife is designed primarily for shaping milled lumber, not for debarking logs. Use a knife with a long, curved blade (see illustration on page 125) with the curve of the blade turned away from the curve of the log. When drawknifing, work with the log about waist height or slightly lower. You can make supports to hold the logs while you work on them by sinking two posts into the ground, and notching them on top to cradle each end of the log.

What will help you most, whether you sap-peel or drawknife, is how well you have limbed the tree beforehand. The secret is not only to cut the limb flush to the tree, but also to dig in below the surface of the trunk slightly and dig the knot out with the nose (the tip) of your chain saw, somewhat like getting the eye out of a potato. This is important because the knot is much harder than the rest of the wood, and if it sticks up at all it will catch

With a Dutch hoe, a common garden tool, you can peel the bark from red pine logs— without bending over.

your drawknife or peeling spade every time and hold you up considerably.

If you are going to haul the logs to your building site right away, leave the bark on to protect them. Bark should be removed soon after you have got your logs to the site, however, to prevent wood-boring

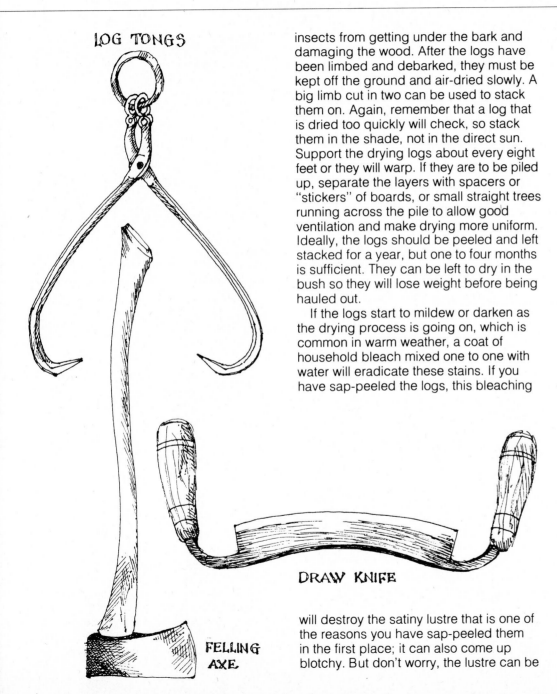

LOG TONGS

DRAW KNIFE

FELLING
AXE

insects from getting under the bark and damaging the wood. After the logs have been limbed and debarked, they must be kept off the ground and air-dried slowly. A big limb cut in two can be used to stack them on. Again, remember that a log that is dried too quickly will check, so stack them in the shade, not in the direct sun. Support the drying logs about every eight feet or they will warp. If they are to be piled up, separate the layers with spacers or "stickers" of boards, or small straight trees running across the pile to allow good ventilation and make drying more uniform. Ideally, the logs should be peeled and left stacked for a year, but one to four months is sufficient. They can be left to dry in the bush so they will lose weight before being hauled out.

If the logs start to mildew or darken as the drying process is going on, which is common in warm weather, a coat of household bleach mixed one to one with water will eradicate these stains. If you have sap-peeled the logs, this bleaching will destroy the satiny lustre that is one of the reasons you have sap-peeled them in the first place; it can also come up blotchy. But don't worry, the lustre can be restored by rubbing in some linseed oil with a rag. To prevent discoloring right after peeling, the logs can also be sprayed or brushed with a solution of one part sodium pentachloraphenate (the active ingredient in most wood preservatives) to three parts water.

When building with the long log method of construction, you can build with green logs. As a matter of fact, the walls of a house are considered a good place for logs to dry, as long as they get a chance to dry slowly. However, if you intend to build in the summer with green logs, to move into the house in the fall and have the furnace on all winter, then you had better steel yourself for the appearance of huge checks in your beautiful logs by the time spring rolls around. A furnace dries the air and acts as a kind of kiln drier, sucking the moisture out of the wood at a rate greater on the inside of the house than on the outside, and much faster than green wood can handle without a great amount of checking and splitting.

Buying the Logs

This could prove to be expensive, but if you just want to build and not get involved with a logging operation, it's probably your best bet. It may even prove to be cheaper if you add in the value of the time in cutting the logs yourself.

Go to a logger, mill, local farmer or log builder and negotiate with them. Tell them how many logs you want, good straight logs of whatever diameter at the butt (thickest) end that you have decided to work with. Have the logs delivered to your building site as you would any other building material such as bricks or sawn boards. The smaller the company you deal with, the better chance you have of getting what you want. This is especially true of the big round structural timbers used for the flowing joint roof system. You might have to cut these yourself and buy only the wall logs. A big company might not want to bother picking out from their bush logs that would be good for you. A small logging operation is a good place to get logs at the source at wholesale prices. Remember that when you are building long log, the length of the building is limited by the length of the logs you can get your hands on. It would be best, of course, if you could pick out your own logs from a logger's bush, because normally they are cut into 8- or 16-foot lengths by the time they get to the yard. Look for straight ones without too much taper. A 35-foot log that is, perhaps, 13 inches at the butt end and tapers down to about 9 inches at the top, is considered an excellent log for building purposes, especially in the eastern part of North America; an eight-inch top is minimum.

Builders who live in the West have huge fir and red cedar — bigger and straighter logs to work with.

Logs that have been bought and delivered will still have to be drawknifed, unless you buy them already mechanically debarked. In our opinion, machine peeling gives the logs a very unattractive appearance and isn't worth the time saved.

Old Barn Logs

Using old barn logs means using tight, well-seasoned material. Because our ancestors had more to choose from, these logs are usually straighter than those you are likely to get from today's bush. You also stand a better chance of getting cedar, a good wood to use because of its resistance to decay and its insulation properties.

On the negative side, buying an old barn is an increasingly disappearing option for most people because of the

End view of scribed and V-grooved logs showing the V's stuffed with insulation.

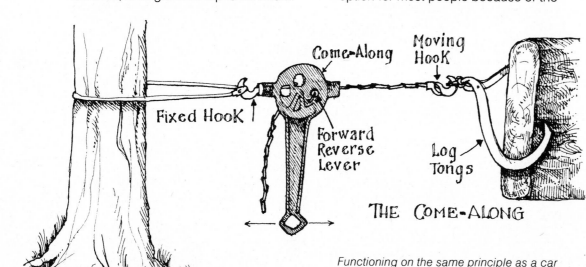

Fixed Hook

Come-Along

Moving Hook

Forward Reverse Lever

Log Tongs

THE COME-ALONG

Functioning on the same principle as a car jack, this device will enable you to exert over a ton of force with only minor effort. Very useful for pulling your truck out of the mud!

finite number of old log buildings, and their popularity as a building material. Hidden spikes and wire can ruin chain saw teeth, and checked surfaces can be hard to scribe. The weathered appearance of the logs drives most people to drawknifing them, and rotten sections might make long log use impossible. The length of the barn governs the length of your building so an old barn that is not very long or has some rotten sections might be best suited for the piece-on-piece style of building which is discussed later in this chapter.

One more thing that might make you reconsider using old barn logs is that they sometimes retain some of those barnyard smells, even after they have been cleaned and installed as logs in your brand-new house.

A fine example of the long log method, this house near Pembroke has the protruding corners of the walls arching at the top and a "bell cast" roof.

LONG LOG

The cutting edge of new log construction methods is the "long log," or Scandinavian, style of log building. These are its three basic features:

1. *Scribing:* The wall logs and structural joints are fitted together by using scribes (basically a pair of dividers) to trace the contours of the top of one log onto the bottom of another.

2. *V-grooving:* The bottom of the logs are grooved out along the scribe lines in the shape of a "V," and stuffed with insulation to prevent drafts from getting through. This V-grooving provides a stable base for the logs to sit on, and also prevents water

from getting in. If the logs were completely round on the bottom, water could run around under the log and remain there rotting it. However, water can't flow up the sharp angle of the V-groove.

3. *Saddle Notch Corners:* This is a notch that sheds water well and is comparatively easy to make. It also has a natural look that goes nicely with the round logs. (See photograph on page 15.)

The long log method of construction gives you a solid, low maintenance log wall that keeps the wind out and has no mortared chinks to be replaced or repaired over the years. Because there is no hewing, the full width of the log is kept, maximizing its insulation properties, whereas you lose some of this with a hewn log.

A number of long log builders we know have dispensed totally with the hewing axe in favour of the chain saw and scribe. Every wall log, plate, rafter and joist is a round log, and where they meet a flowing joint is made. With this type of joinery a

Logs flow together at the corners as though they grew that way. Joints such as this present a striking contrast to the normal building techniques of sharp corners and straight lines.

feel for the chain saw, a tool not normally thought of as precise, must be developed. The result is a house where all the pieces seem to grow out of each other with a feeling of solid integration that approaches sculpture.

JOINING THE SILL LOGS TO THE FOUNDATION

For your two sill logs, choose the straightest logs you have of a slightly

At home with the wilderness that surrounds it, this hand-made home leaves nothing owing at the bank. The owner built the original part of the house from logs found on his own property, though he found that they were too rough and sharply tapered to permit a first-rate job. When adding the new wing to accommodate his growing family, he decided to buy larger and more uniform red pine.

above average thickness. Cut them to the exact desired length.

You will want to flatten the bottoms just enough that they will sit flat and stable on the foundation. To do this decide how much you want to take off and measure down from the center of the log ends this amount. Snap a chalk line along the length of the log from these points at both ends. The line must always be pulled in the same plane that the saw cut will follow. Do not pull it at right angles to the saw

Normally, window and door openings are cut out of the completed log walls. However, more economical use of the logs can be made by using short filler logs between the openings as the walls go up. Four sharpened pieces of reinforcing rod can be driven in to keep the logs in place while they are being scribed.

Notice the strip of styrofoam that has been sandwiched between the sill log and the foundation.

cut. Roll the log until the line is in the right position so that if the saw blade is held vertical, it will cut through the desired plane. Score the line first with your chain saw nose, then make the full cut all the way through the log, keeping your saw blade vertical at all times.

The two gable end sill logs which run between the sill logs, and complete the square are cut flat so that their thickness is about one-half the thickness of the sill logs. They are cut to length so their ends extend into notches cut in the underside of the sill logs.

Lay the logs up on the foundation with their tapers running in opposite directions. Mark the center of mass of the tops of all four logs with chalk lines. The logs are then set so that these lines form an exact square. They are also used as reference points when you are getting the wall to go up plumb. Make sure that the exterior of the foundation does not protrude beyond the sill logs or water will run in. When the sill logs are in place, mark their exact position on the floor and put them aside.

To join the sill logs to the foundation, embed six-inch spikes into mortar poured into the holes of the top blocks, so that about three inches of the points of the spikes are left protruding. Now lay a one-inch-thick piece of styrofoam over the spikes on the foundation. The sill logs are then put back into place and driven down onto the spikes. The styrofoam acts as a seal and a vapor barrier to prevent water from being drawn up from the masonry. It is a good idea to put plastic sheeting or tar paper under the foam to improve this vapor barrier.

If you are not planning to cover the styrofoam with a fascia board on the outside, it would be a good idea to coat the outside of the foam with tar because wood preservatives will dissolve the foam and mice can tunnel through it into the house. Tar alone will do, but covering it with wood is by far the best and neatest solution.

Another way to anchor the sills is to embed reinforcing rods or J-shaped anchor bolts in the foundation about every four feet with the tops protruding a few inches. Line up the sills beside these bars and drill corresponding holes in them so they will drop in place over the bars.

SCRIBES

As we have mentioned, scribes are a pair of dividers which transfer the contours of the top of one log onto the bottom of another. When the first log is grooved out along these lines, it fits perfectly onto the log below it. Some scribes have divergent metal points to scrape the line onto the log, others have an attachment on one arm for a pencil. If you use a pencil, experiment with different colors and types. A 6-B artist's pencil works well; it's soft and leaves a good mark, even on a wet log, although it does tend to break and wear out quickly. If you prefer a pencil that lasts longer, you could use one with indelible lead; the mark is not as clear as with a soft pencil, but if you lose this line, wet it and it will show up again. Felt-tip pens, we have found, are not very reliable.

A frame "knee wall" gives added head space in the second floor. In this case the central pair of purlins are for decoration.

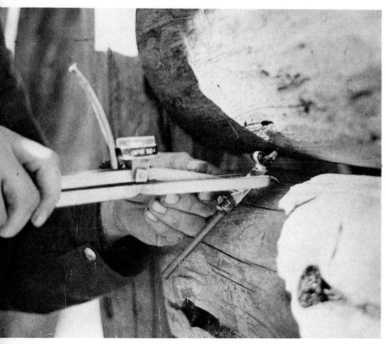

A pair of log scribes with a pencil attachment. These scribes also have divergent points for greater accuracy.

The above photograph shows a pair of home-made scribes with divergent points, a pencil attachment and a bubble level mounted on top. This level is very important because it gives you a fixed, horizontal plane to move your scribes along. If the scribe arms are not kept level, the line you are tracing onto a log will move, either up or down, in relation to the plane on which you started, making your line so inaccurate that the log won't drop plumb on the log below it. The bubble level is a reference point for checking and correcting the line you are scribing, keeping it the same all the way along the log.

PUTTING THE WALLS UP

The place to begin all these procedures is the pile of wall logs that you have picked and stacked together. Pick out a log with the idea of matching it with the log that will be below it in the wall. The goal is to have every second round close to horizontally level. For example, if the sill log has a lot of taper, the log above it should also taper. This way you can alternate the taper and keep the wall level every second round.

The sequence shown in the photographs took seven hours to complete, but the time was well worth it — the result is spectacular. The time could have been reduced considerably, however, by using straighter and more uniform logs. These scribing and notching procedures are also used to make the flowing notches and joints shown on page 143.

The final log, which is called the wall plate log, is the one that the roof rafters will sit on. It is extremely important that this log will be horizontally level so the roof will not be crooked. Unlevel wall plates make roof building very difficult and frustrating.

Your sill and wall plate logs should be the straightest logs that you have. Get the wall plate up on the wall and position it where you want it to sit. Determine when the top of it will be level by measuring down to the floor as in the photo on page 133, and put blocks under the log to hold

The finished house with Mansard roof and Dutch "hex" door.

Another view of the frame knee-wall.

it in this position. Now measure the space between the logs at both ends, and scribe off the corresponding amount from each rough saddle notch. This will bring the log level. When doing the final scribing for the V-groove in the bottom of the plate, remember that the plates on each side of the house should end up at the same height.

As is customary in log work, the plate is pinned to the two or three rounds of logs below it with wooden pegs or steel bars. (See Chapter 3.)

DOORS AND WINDOWS

The height of the windows you put in should be decided before the building is started. You are going to have to cut into the log above and below the window opening in order to set your windows in. It will be best if the top and bottom of the opening occur at a point half way (or slightly less) through the respective log. Start thinking about this when you get to within a couple of feet of the window so that you can arrive at the right height for the bottom window log without having to scribe off too much of it, as can sometimes happen.

A slot is cut into the sides of the window openings big enough to take a 2- x 4-inch spline which is wrapped in fiberglass (see photo on page 139) to make a seal, and is hammered into the slot, extending about 3/4 inch into the bottom window sill log and up into the top cap log. This top cap log also has a slot cut up into it directly over the spline so that when the logs shrink and settle, the spline will go up into the slot in the cap log allowing the log wall to settle down around it. Use the formula of 3/4 inch of shrinkage per foot of rough opening height for green logs to calculate the depth of the slots in the cap logs and the space allowed between the window frame top and the log above.

The frames that the windows sit in are nailed to the splines, not to the logs. Doors are done the same way, except that the slots are made deeper because there is more height and therefore more shrinkage.

V-Notching and Scribing

1. *Carry the log you have picked over to the wall and hoist it up on top. (See cant hooks in the illustration on page 91.) The log should be placed "belly up," that is, with any bow or warp curving up so that it will sit stable when you roll it over on the wall to work on it.*

Position the log exactly where you want it to sit on the wall. Lining up the exact centers of the butt ends will not always be enough, as the logs are irregular and often slightly bowed. The center of the mass of the whole log is what you are concerned with. This is determined visually by standing back and taking a look. Check the whole wall with a spirit level periodically, and a straight edge board to make sure that no optical illusions are affecting your opinion of what looks vertical.

2. *The surfaces of the logs which the scribe lines will pass over are trimmed of all knots and humps with a chain saw then smoothed out with a wood rasp that resembles a small cheese grater on a handle. This is done so the scribes will have a relatively smooth surface to go over. As much of this trimming as possible is done on the ground before the log is raised onto the wall. The logs used for the building shown in the following photos are dry spruce bought from a logging operation.*

3. *This photo shows a log "dog" being driven into the wall and a log which is being worked on. When you have positioned the log where you want it on the wall and before you begin to scribe it, "dog" it in place so it can't move.*

4. Measure down from the top of the log to the floor at several points along its length to check the level, or angle of lay. By varying the depth of the rough saddle notches or by placing wedges under the low end, the log is brought to the desired level for final scribing. When selecting the log, choosing its level of lay and deciding how much is to be scribed off, remember that every second round should be close to level on its top side and close to the same height on both sides of the building. It is always necessary to be aware of the size of the next round of logs at the corners to avoid some difficult joinery problems. You must not cut the saddle notch and V-groove so deep that the log will be weakened or be cut away to nothing at the small end. At the same time the notch and V-groove of any log should not be so shallow that the notch which sits on top of it will require a cut-out arc of more than 180 degrees in order for the log's bottom to touch the log below. If the arc is more than 180 degrees, the opening will start to become smaller and won't fit over the log it is to sit on.

5. The rough saddle notches are scribed on each end of the log where it rests on the wall log that is below, and runs at right angles to it. These rough notches are cut to bring the logs closer together so the scribes will work right. The final notches will be done later. Measure the gap between the two logs on each end and set your scribes to a width that is a little less than this so there will be no chance of the logs touching or hanging up. If necessary, the size of the rough notch may be different for each end of the log to adjust the level of it. Run the scribers over the top of the supporting log, transferring its contours onto the log you are working on. Do this on the inside and the outside then roll the log over onto the adjacent walls. Now carefully trace these scribed lines with the nose of your chain saw.

6. Make a cut in the center of the rough saddle notch to the full depth of the notch.

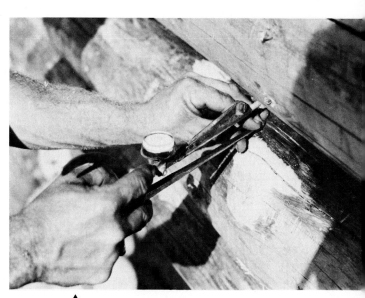

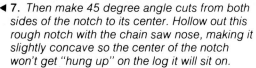

▲
◄ **7.** *Then make 45 degree angle cuts from both sides of the notch to its center. Hollow out this rough notch with the chain saw nose, making it slightly concave so the center of the notch won't get "hung up" on the log it will sit on.*

▲
8. *Put the log back in place and drive the dog back in to hold it still. This is the time to cut the log to its final length. Set your scribes to the widest gap between the logs and add about half an inch or more, depending on where you have decided the log should sit (see step #4). When using scribes with a bubble level and adjustable pencil attachment, adjust the length of the pencil so that when they are held with the bubble showing level, the tips will be vertical. This is done by holding the points to a spirit level which is held plumb and adjusting the length of the pencil until the bubble on the scribes shows level.*

◄ **9.** *Run the bottom arm of the scribes along the full length of the top of the lower log and the pencil will trace its contours onto the bottom of the log above. Do this on the inside and the outside of the log and around the saddle notches. Remember to keep the scribes level by checking the bubble level mounted on top.*

At the butt ends of the log scribe the contour of the top of the lower log onto the butt end of the upper log. This is done so that the first six inches or so of the groove can be formed with the nose of the chain saw rather than having the full V-groove continue right to the end and be visible. Now roll the log onto the adjacent walls so the bottom is facing up.

10. *Go over the scribed pencil line with a chisel or a knife. This chiseled line will stop any chips from splitting past your scribed line. The line and about the first 1/8 inch of wood are not touched until you are finished V-grooving.*

11. *With the log turned 180 degrees from its final resting position and the chain saw in a vertical position follow your scribe line (but don't touch it) cutting to a depth of 1/2 to 1 inch. These shallow guide cuts are made because it is much easier to follow the winding scribe line with the nose of the saw than it would be with the saw embedded far enough to cut the full V-groove. The guide cut is wide enough to allow the full V-cut to be made on a much straighter course as it can be further away from the scribe line.*

12. *Now you can groove out the end of the log following the line scribed there in step #9. This short round groove can be seen on the log end in this photo and the one following. Note once again that both the guide cut and the V-groove cut start after the end grooves.*

Now on the end of the log draw a check mark (√) which will represent the final cut. This should be no deeper than necessary to ensure that the log will rest only on the edges of the groove, which should be as shallow as possible. Now turn the log so that one of the V-lines is plumb vertical, as shown.

15. *The final saddle notch being cut in the same manner that the rough notch was cut in the previous photographs, though more carefully as this is the final cut.*

13. *With one of the V-pattern lines vertical and the saw held in a vertical position, make the full V-cut along the length of the log to the depth indicated by the V-pattern on the end. Depth can be controlled by eye or by a mark made on the chain bar with a grease pencil. Once again do not touch the original scribe line with the saw. Turn the log until the other V-pattern line is vertical, and make the second cut. You will have now cut out a V-shaped channel in the bottom of the log.*

14. *This photo shows the chain saw trimming off the point that remains between the initial shallow cut and the full V-cut.*

16. *The ¹/₈ inch of wood that is left on the inside of the chiseled scribe line is carefully trimmed off up to the line. (A linoleum knife works well for this.)*

17. *The same trimming with a knife is done to the saddle notch. Here is the finished notch. Note once again that the entire center is dished slightly to prevent protruding pieces from "hanging up" the log. Only the outside edges of the notch ride on the log below.*

18. *The finished log is rolled into place to check its fit. This one fit perfectly the first time, but some may need a bit of trimming. Once the log is a satisfactory fit, it is rolled back and stuffed with insulation before being put finally in place.*

This complicated house was built by only two men, aided in their formidable task by the use of winches and cable trollies. Note how they have positioned the rafters over the right hand gable end in a novel and functional way of achieving a wide gable overhang.

Cutting out the channel for the sliding splines to which the window units are fastened.

The same house. The log ends on the right have been cut to form a doorless passage way. In this situation the builders stopped cutting the V-groove a few inches before the butt ends were reached and dished out the remainder of the log with the nose of the chain saw, the same treatment as for exterior corners (see step #12 on page 135.) As a result, the unsightly V-grooves which appear on the butts of the logs of the rough door opening to the left are not seen.

The logs on the left are prepared for the installation of an exterior door frame. A 2 x 4 which the door frame will be nailed to has been inserted in a channel cut vertically in the log ends. The logs will slide on this 2 x 4 as they settle downward during shrinkage and settling of the building. The cavity cut in the log above the top of the 2 x 4 is to allow the 2 x 4 to slide up as the building settles.

A close-up of log ends grooved out to accept a sliding nailer to which a window or door frame will be anchored. If you look closely at the radical cracks in the log ends you will see how easily water can enter the logs as it runs down the exterior wall during a rain. The damage and decay which this will cause must be combated by building a wide overhang and by periodically caulking the offending cracks and applying a preservative to the logs.

This staircase has its treads angled forward slightly and is hinged at the top. This is done so that the staircase can come down and straighten up as the house shrinks and settles. A much simpler method is to put a series of blocks underneath the staircase and knock them out when necessary.

This cathedral roof, supported by beautiful roof trusses, illustrates how you could easily find worthwhile the considerable extra work and expense required in their construction.

Piece-on-piece

Basically, the piece-on-piece method involves the construction of a post-and-beam frame, using either round or squared timbers. The plates and sill logs comprise the beams, and the posts are the vertical studs. The studs are slotted to receive the short, horizontal filler logs that fill the gaps in the wall between them. The filler logs can then be scribed and V-grooved as in the long log method described previously. Of course once a post-and-beam frame has been built, it can be filled with all kinds of materials, such as stone, board and batten, vertical logs (known as stockade style — an impractical method because it is impossible to keep the logs sealed as they shrink and expand), and firewood-sized logs

Time, patience and untold hours of work have transformed the remains of two dilapidated old log barns into this grand piece-on-piece house. The three-foot thick basement walls are local stone fitted and mortared in place, and the owner's own bush provided the poles for the roof.

mortared into place (see the following Stackwall section, page 152).

The piece-on-piece style was used to a certain extent in the Thirteen Colonies and in early Canadian settlement, and even reached Western settlements, where it was known as "Red River" (or "Manitoba frame") construction.

It is a good method to consider if you can't get long, straight, building logs. With piece-on-piece, the logs used for the walls have to be only as long as the distance between the wall posts, and this distance is up to you. Pieces cut from long logs, unsuitable for other purposes because of curves, can be used as filler logs. Another advantage of piece-on-piece is that it is modular. This means that different teams of people can work on several sections at once. On the other hand, if there is a shortage of manpower, even one builder working alone can erect a substantially sized house, because the units are small and easy to handle. Wall directions can be changed easily by simply slotting the wall post on the side that you want the wall to extend from, and on any angle that you want. You can build an interesting and intricately walled house that changes wall directions often. The same applies to interior log partitions which can be made this way more easily than notching in dovetails or saddle notches into the wall. However, the difficulty of the layout and joinery required recommends this style to only the experienced and patient builder if a tight, high-quality house is your aim.

ORGANIZATION

With piece-on-piece, the precutting and organization of the different component pieces can take as long as one week, but it is worth it in the long run because of the time saved later. Draw up a tally sheet of how many logs you will need, and the sizes they should be. Choose the most difficult-to-find first. As with the long log method, these will be the structural members — the plates, sills, studs, ridge poles, etc. They have to be the straightest and the longest, so select them first, label them and put them aside.

When you come to a long log that you don't want for a structural piece, you can cut out a length that you will need for a filler log. A convenient length for these filler logs is eight feet because many saw logs are cut to eight-foot lengths by saw mills and many building materials are manufactured with a 4- x 8-foot format in mind. You could use a stand of trees that taper too much after eight feet, or order logs from a mill or cedar post yard. If you have a twenty-foot log with a straight piece in it that is straight for sixteen feet and then curves, you could cut out two eight-foot filler logs. The four feet that you have left can be used for a short filler log to go between a window and a stud. Look for particular things as you search through your log pile. If, for instance, you like thick,

vertical studs, a structural and aesthetic taste, and you see something thick and straight and of the right length in a particular log, cut it out for a stud. Studs are usually thicker than filler logs. Tick all these pieces off on your tally sheet and stack them together, each with its own kind, so that you can find them quickly when you need them — even if it snows.

ATTACHING THE VERTICAL WALL STUD TO THE SILL LOG

Once you have attached the sill log to the foundation by following the same steps as for the long log method (page 128), you then attach the studs to the sill log. The essence of building with round logs is that you are building with center lines (the center of the total mass of the log), so the first thing to do is to chalk line the center of the sill log and lay out the position of the studs on it. Cut out a rough mortise in the sill where the vertical stud will sit. Use a plywood jig (pattern) for this. If the sill log is big enough to take it, you could make this jig one chain saw bar wide and one-and-a-half long; if not, you will have to make it smaller, and use a chisel and hammer.

Now find the center of the vertical stud on its end. If the log is not very round, you might have a false center if you rely solely on measurement, so use a combination of "eyeballing" and measuring. Again, you are looking for the center of the mass. This is an important part of log building — take your time and do it right. Using these center points on the ends, quarter the stud with lines snapped on with a chalk line, taking them right over the ends and up the sides so that the entire stud is quartered. Put cross hairs on your plywood mortise jig, line them up with the lines quartering

the bottom of the stud, and use the jig to mark out a tenon on the bottom of the stud. Make the tenon slightly smaller than the mortise. This joint is made primarily to keep the stud from moving laterally only, and shouldn't be made too tight because you will be taking the stud out of the sill periodically during the following procedures.

Brace the stud temporarily in its final vertical position. You are now ready to scribe the stud onto the sill, using the method shown in step #5 on page 133. After this notch has been scribed you should wait until the stud has been V-notched before you cut it.

An alternative to this scribed notch is to flatten the sill log on the top, and have a flat bottom on the stud with the same mortise in the sill and the same tenon in the stud. This method is easier, but it doesn't look as good. Also, because it is a flat joint, it will let water collect on the sill under the stud. The beauty of a house built with scribed notches is that water never gets a chance to collect anywhere, because the notched surfaces slope downward.

V-NOTCHING THE POST

Log builders are still searching for the perfect method of notching the filler logs into the vertical studs. There probably isn't a perfect system, and we have illustrated four that we have found in use. In this chapter, we will use the one shown in the illustration on the opposite page, second from the top.

Make two triangular plywood templates with center lines on them that are the shape you want the notches in the post to be. Some builders use an angle of about 120 degrees at the triangle top. Since you will be making a notch on each side of the

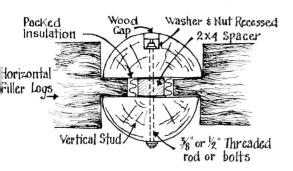

Packed Insulation — Wood Cap — Washer & Nut Recessed — 2×4 Spacer

Horizontal Filler Logs

Vertical Stud — ⅜" or ½" Threaded rod or bolts

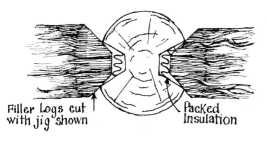

Filler Logs cut with jig shown — Packed Insulation

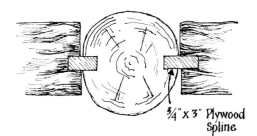

¾" × 3" Plywood Spline

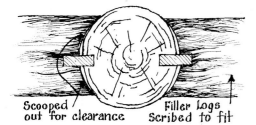

Scooped out for clearance — Filler Logs Scribed to fit

FOUR DETAILS OF FILLER LOGS JOINING VERTICAL STUDS IN PIECE-ON-PIECE STYLE

Detail of a wall stud scribed onto a sill log—a flowing joint.

stud, the V-notch shouldn't be too deep or it will weaken the log. Tack the two plywood templates onto both butt ends of the stud so that the center lines of the triangles line up with the center lines you put on the stud and the triangle points are an equal distance from their respective centers. (See the illustration on the following page.) This distance is relative to the size of the individual stud. Put on two chalk lines which will connect the points where the triangle sides intersect with the extreme edge of the stud butt end. Pull the chalk line at the same angle that the saw blade will be in when cutting.

The inside of this saddle notch should be cupped or dished very slightly around the tenon, with a gouge or the nose of a chain saw, so that only the outside of the notch will rest on the sill. Then shim up the notch in the center so all the weight will not be on the outside of the notch, which

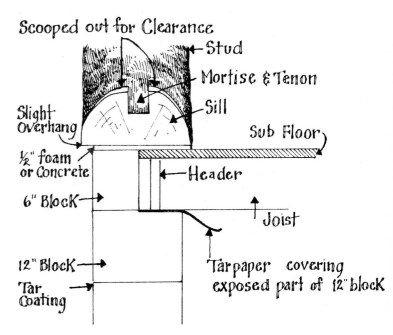

DETAIL OF WALL STUD MEETING SILL LOG

Scooped out for Clearance — Stud

Mortise & Tenon

Sill

Slight Overhang

Sub Floor

½" foam or Concrete

6" Block — Header

Joist

12" Block

Tar Coating — Tarpaper covering exposed part of 12" block

might cause the stud to split. Repeat this process for the V-notch on the opposite side of the stud. After the V-notch lines have been marked on, you should cut out the base of the stud where it was previously scribed to fit over the sill.

Now you can cut out the V-notches. First score the lines with a shallow cut of your chain saw. Make your final cuts by turning the log, so that one line is centered and the side of the triangular templates plumb. Cut with your saw in a vertical position. Estimate the depth of the cut by using your triangular templates as guides. You could also put a mark on the chain saw bar at the depth you want to cut. This doesn't have to be perfectly accurate as long as you don't cut too deep and weaken the stud. Try to leave about eight inches between the points of the V cuts. Neither does this notch have to be exactly plumb when standing vertical in the wall, but if it is not you must measure the distance between the inside of the V-notches before each filler log is cut and change the length of each filler log to match.

Place the stud in its final position and brace it in all four directions to stop it from moving as the filler pieces go in. You will have realized by now log work involves a lot of visual centering because logs don't have a steady contour. So eyeball the vertical post from different angles, and get a second opinion from someone with a good eye. It's much like hanging a picture.

CUTTING THE FILLER LOG ENDS

To cut the ends of the filler logs, use slightly broader triangular templates than were used to mark the studs to ensure a tight fit (see illustration on page 143, left, second from top). Tack them to the ends of a board, exactly the same distance apart as the distance between the inside of the notches of the vertical studs. This new template is placed on top of each filler log and used as a guide to cut the points on the ends, as explained on page 146.

Now slide the filler log down between the studs, using a sledge hammer if necessary to get them down. Overly-tight-fitting filler logs could push the studs out. It might be necessary to take the filler logs out of the wall to adjust their length. Make sure the studs are plumb as you go along, and alternate the taper of the filler logs to keep the wall level. How long you spend on these joints is up to you. Between one and ten hours could be spent on each one, and the result will

Close-up detail of a corner stud where it meets the sill logs.

depend on how much time you put into it.

Once you are satisfied that the filler log is sitting properly, you can scribe it to fit over the log below. Set your scribes to the widest gap between the two logs and add a little for insurance. Scribe it and V-groove it using the same method described in the Long Log section. Pack insulation into the V-groove, as well as into the gap between the sawed-off point of the filler log end and the V-notch in the post.

It's important to remember to drill holes in the filler logs for wiring as you go along. All this has to be planned beforehand.

There is a quick alternative to scribing and V-notching that we have seen, but would not recommend for a home, although it will serve well for a utility building or garage. It consists of setting all the logs in the wall, getting them as close together as possible, then running a chain saw between them until their edges meet. Pry them apart and put a layer of insulation

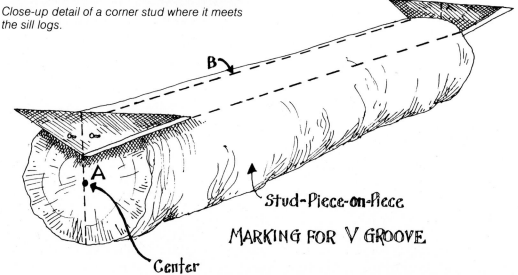

Stud-Piece-on-Piece

MARKING FOR V GROOVE

Center

and bead of caulking in between each log, then tap the top of the wall with a sledge hammer to bring them all down tight. The small cracks may have to be mortared or caulked afterwards, but this is a very fast method for putting up a barn or a shed.

When working with logs you are working with a variable material. Some forethought is required to arrive at the right place with the right log. For instance, the top filler log has to come up to the right height in order to fit under the plate log without having to scribe off half the log to accomplish this. Estimate how high you want your walls to be and how much average elevation per log you will get after scribing. The house in the photo on page 141 was built out of old barn logs and has a wall height of 8 feet 10½ inches, with an average gain of elevation per log of 10 inches — that is, a 12-inch log with an average of 2 inches scribed off.

PUTTING THE PLATE LOG ON

If you wanted to (or had to), you could put the top plate log on immediately after the posts were up and braced, making the structure rigid and enabling you to put a roof on it. This would be necessary in case you wanted to work under shelter during bad weather. Since the logs can't be put in from the top when the plate is on, slots have to be cut in the top of the studs in order to slide the filler logs into the wall. These slots will have to be patched up later and this patched effect doesn't look the best. Another factor to consider when putting the roof on first is that when working with a rigid structure your tolerances are smaller and your scope of

Piece-on-Piece house near Sharbot Lake.

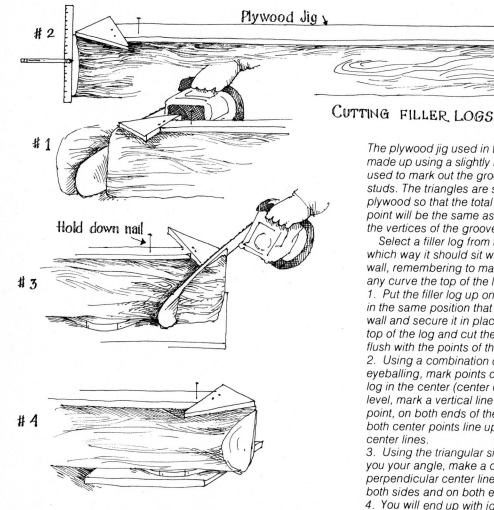

Plywood Jig

2

1

Hold down nail

3

4

CUTTING FILLER LOGS

The plywood jig used in the following steps is made up using a slightly broader angle than was used to mark out the grooves in the upright studs. The triangles are screwed to a length of plywood so that the total length from point to point will be the same as the distance between the vertices of the grooves in the upright studs.

Select a filler log from the pile and decide which way it should sit when in place in the wall, remembering to make the convex side of any curve the top of the log.

1. Put the filler log up on blocks or saw horses in the same position that it will finally take in the wall and secure it in place. Nail the jig on the top of the log and cut the log ends square and flush with the points of the jig.

2. Using a combination of measurement and eyeballing, mark points on the butt ends of the log in the center (center of mass). Using a spirit level, mark a vertical line through that center point, on both ends of the log. Move the jig so both center points line up with their respective center lines.

3. Using the triangular side of the jig to give you your angle, make a cut following the perpendicular center line downward. Do this on both sides and on both ends of the log.

4. You will end up with identical arrow-shaped points at both ends of the log. The points will be parallel and the angles of the points will be the same in relation to the horizontal center of the log.

operations narrower. For instance, you couldn't scribe the plate log onto the top filler logs. For this reason, we don't recommend doing this, at least not for piece-on-piece construction.

The conventional way to proceed is to wait until all the walls are put up, then put the wall plate on. It is structurally desirable to have a single plate run the entire length

of the building, but two logs can be spliced together for this purpose. (See illustration on page 147.)

Get the plate into position on the wall

and block up the low end until the top is level (as shown on page 147, bottom center). It should be one of your longest and straightest logs. The top of the plate log *must* be level in order for the rafters to sit properly so that the roof won't be crooked. If you have cross beams spanning the width of the building to hold the walls together, you will want them to sit on top of the posts, and have the plate log saddle notched right over top of them. Mark and cut out rough saddle notches in the bottom of the plate directly over these cross beams in order to bring the plate down to close scribing tolerances. You can then scribe and V-groove the wall plate so it sits down over the top filler logs, the cross beams and the two logs it will sit on at either end. The plate log is also packed with insulation, and pegged through the cross beams and into the stud. Use the same one-inch auger bit and drill extension described in Chapter 3, and a one-inch steel bar for a peg. You will also have to V-notch the cross beams so that the ends of the top filler logs will fit into them.

THE GAP PROBLEM

With piece-on-piece construction, you have free-floating horizontal logs settling down between the vertical studs. This happens because the horizontal filler logs shrink through their thickness, while the vertical studs do not shrink along their length. In time this will form a gap under the plate log. You could spike the filler logs to the studs to stop the accumulative gap from forming under the plate, but that would create a smaller gap between each log that would have to be dealt with separately, probably by mortaring or caulking, the very steps that scribing

PIECE-ON-PIECE
WALL SECTION

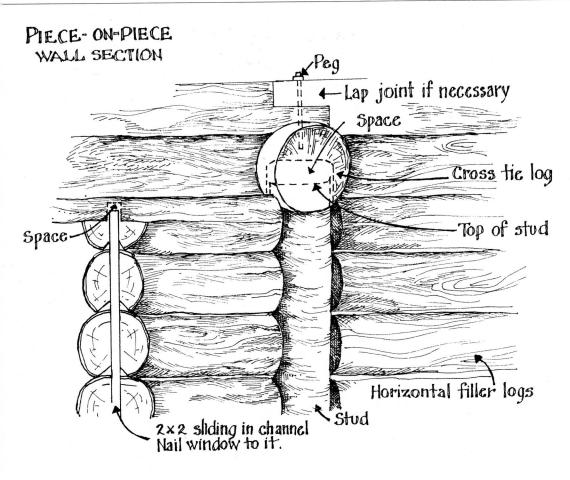

- Peg
- ← Lap joint if necessary
- Space
- Cross tie log
- Top of stud
- Space
- Horizontal filler logs
- Stud
- 2×2 sliding in channel. Nail window to it.

is supposed to eliminate. By now you can see how it would help to use well-seasoned logs when building piece-on-piece to minimize this gap.

Probably the easiest way to fill the gap is to stuff it with insulation and nail a fascia board, a good quality pine board, over the gap once it has shrunk about as much as it is going to. This board could also be a round log ripped in half and nailed on with the round side facing out in order to blend with the appearance of the wall.

By far the best, but also the most labor-intensive, method of reducing the gap is to cut wells (spaces) into the bottom of the plate log or cross-tie logs, as shown in the illustration on this page.

Another method of sealing the gap is the key spline that is shown in the illustration below.

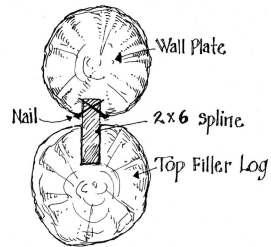

- Wall Plate
- Nail
- 2×6 spline
- Top Filler Log

SLIDING SPLINE WEATHER SEAL

◄ Sketch showing the top wall plate of a piece-on-piece building in place for scribing. Rough notches have been cut in the plate to make it level and to bring it down close enough to the logs below it to be scribed.

If a space is cut in the bottom of the horizontal cross tie log, the vertical wall stud will be able to slide up into that space as the building settles during drying. This will allow the whole building to settle as a unit rather than having the filler log sections settle individually, causing a space to form in the wall at the top of each section. Remember that vertical log members do not loose height during drying as the horizontal logs do. If well-seasoned logs are used this detail will be unnecessary.

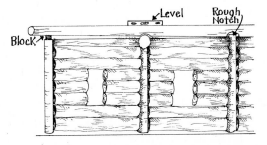

- Level
- Rough Notch
- Block

LEVELING WALL PLATE

The eaves of this roof illustrate the difficulty which we discussed earlier of insulating an exposed beam roof. The pole rafters of this house are quite sufficient to hold the roof, but to leave them showing on the interior it has been necessary to add a further complete frame of 2 x 10s to contain the fiberglass insulation. Fascia boards will eventually cover the exposed ends.

The poles protruding from the gable ends support the floor of the loft. Those larger poles protruding from the front of the house both tie together the opposite walls of the house and provide support for the floor joists of the second level.

Close-up detail of the front wall.

The log gable at the eaves.

Mason's line can be seen strung across the roof at various points. These lines are used to establish correct height of the rafter top when scribing rafters over purlins.

Detail of wall plate and rafter support.

Both the materials and the design of this house convey a sense of solid security. The wall logs are not V-grooved to fit over each other, rather they have been made to fit together by running a chain saw between them to remove the high points. The owner-builder says that V-grooving would have been preferable as the joints are not sufficiently air-tight and must now be chinked.

One spring, three new arrivals to the bush country decided to build a log house (shown on page 150, top right) on 100 acres of cooperatively owned land. Their combined knowledge of mechanical engineering, construction techniques, and common sense, produced good results. They were originally going to build a long log style of house, using spruce and balsam cut out of their own bush. But the trees had too much taper for long log, so they chose to build in the piece-on-piece style and still use their own trees. Cutting started in April and was finished in June — the month when the woods are alive with blackflies and other maddening insects. They told horror stories of how they sweated under layers of buttoned-up clothing and bee-keepers' hats. They vow that next time they will do the logging in

the winter. It was a very time-consuming process — a neighbor skidded the logs out for them with his horses. But it was well worth it when you consider that the total cost of the logs was practically zero, if you don't count their time, which was considerable. Altogether, a total of eighty trees were cut for their 32- x 24-foot house.

First, a concrete pad was poured and re-bar (reinforcing rod) was embedded around the periphery to go through holes in the sill log and attach them to the foundation. Next they put up studs and the entire roof structure, giving them a rigid frame with spaces between them for the filler logs to go into later. The roof was a post-and-purlin roof system (see page 56) with a ridge pole running along the top. Three triangular-shaped timber trusses, two at each end and one in the middle,

supported the ridge and purlins. Both the purlins and the ridge pole were spliced with a doweled lap joint over the middle truss.

The notching system used for the seven-foot, six-inch-long filler logs is shown in the illustration on page 143 (top). The studs are milled 4- x 6-inch hardwood. The ends of the filler logs were cut with a chain saw down to a four-inch tenon, and slabs (round logs ripped in half) were bolted to both the inside and outside of the stud. This is an excellent method to use if the roof is built first, because all the filler logs can be put in the wall and then the final slab bolted on, completing the notch. These slabs can be taken off if there are any corrections to be made later.

The trees were felled and the filler logs were all scribed and V-grooved with a small (14-inch bar) chain saw; a larger saw was used for ripping.

They started putting the logs up in September and worked eight-hour days. They moved in at the end of November, just as the snow started to fly.

Across the driveway, another of the landowners built a piece-on-piece house (the one seen above). He bought eight-foot logs from a cedar post yard, and also used some cedar telephone poles for his 16- x 24-foot building. Concrete pilings were used for the foundation, that is, four-foot holes were dug in the ground and thick cardboard tubes that can be bought for this purpose were inserted then filled with concrete. Anchor bolts were embedded in the tops of these pillars when the concrete was wet. Corresponding holes were drilled in the sill logs so they would fit over the bolts on top of the pillars.

He used the spline jointing system shown in the illustration on page 143, third down. The studs were logs flattened on two sides with a heavy-duty chain saw and then planed. A channel slightly deeper than 1/2 inch was cut in the inside face of the stud and also in the flattened ends of the filler logs. A one-inch plywood spline was hammered into the channel that was formed by the meeting of the cuts in the stud and filler log ends to hold it all together. The stud was also scribed over, and splined to, the sill log. He thinks that trying to square the log ends is both time consuming and unnecessary, as it was very difficult to make the butt ends of the filler logs square with the studs. This was mostly due to the taper of the cedar logs.

All the logs were scribed and V-grooved on the bottom, as were the top plates which were saddle notched over each other.

He cut wells into the bottom of the plates directly over the studs so the building would settle without leaving a gap, but the wells were not cut wide enough, and the studs didn't settle up into the plate. The resulting gap was ³/₄ inch and he intends to use the triangular scrap that resulted from the V-grooving to plug it up.

The windows had splines inset into the sides of the openings and the frames were nailed to them so that the walls could settle over the windows and he says it worked out very well.

He built a cathedral roof using pole rafters (cut from thin, straight spruce trees), tongue-and-groove cedar boards for the roof sheeting, strapping, insulation and tin roofing.

He did most of the work himself and plans to build an addition soon, only this time using heavier material and employing the scalloped joint system shown in the illustration at the bottom of page 143.

Stackwall pig barn built without a main frame. The owner is pleased with both the economy of the construction and the functioning of the finished product. High levels of interior moisture keep the wall logs swollen reducing the number of cracks which appear.

Stackwall

Sometimes referred to as the "cordwood" or "log butt" method, stackwall construction incorporates short pieces or "blocks" of logs which are laid like bricks with mortar fill between them. A pattern of round butt ends in a background of mortar appears on the inside and outside of the finished wall.

A stackwall workshop built with a 12- × 12-inch timber frame.

ADVANTAGES

1. The main advantage of stackwall is that virtually any kind of tree or log can be used, even trees that don't have any real commercial value. People have built perfectly good houses out of wood that would normally be considered fit only as fuel for the stove. This makes stackwood an ecologically desirable method, since all of the tree can be used, even the limbs.

Because all of the logs used are cut up into short sections, the taper of the tree is irrelevant. Curves, warpage, or rotten spots which would normally make a log unusable for building can be cut out and thrown away, and the remaining pieces used in the wall. For housing in remote areas such as the far north, where bringing in the materials for regular frame housing presents a formidable problem, the stackwall house offers a good alternative. Trees of any shape and quality may be fashioned into sound houses by virtually unskilled workers.

2. There are no heavy logs to lift. Stackwall is a light mechanical process. Anyone can lay blocks and mix mortar.

3. With stackwall, you are not limited in the shape of your buildings. The corners don't have to be square — they can be round, or any weird and wonderful shape your imagination can concoct. The blocks in the wall can be laid in any pattern you want, and the exposed growth rings form beautiful designs on the walls.

4. Stackwall provides a durable and fire-resistant wall. Just think about how hard it would be to start a blazing fire from a wall made of log ends and mortar.

5. Wood has the interesting property of transmitting water vapor from a high to a low humidity zone lengthwise through its end grain, without actually becoming wet itself. This particular property moderates the problem of uncontrolled winter humidity experienced in many well-insulated homes. This water vapor-transmitting quality also makes stackwall excellent for building barns or structures that will house animals.

6. Stackwall can be made insect repellent. The lime in the mortar keeps insects from moving about inside the walls, and wood preservative discourages their entry through the exposed end grain.

DISADVANTAGES

1. The main disadvantage with the stackwall method is that you are using two substances that don't make a perfect seal. Temperature and humidity make wood move more than cement. The wood pulls away from the cement, creating cracks around the blocks that let the wind in and will later have to be caulked extensively. The blocks can sometimes crack right through their length from one end to the other, and these cracks have to be caulked too. These problems can be minimized by proper drying procedures (discussed later in the chapter) but they cannot be eliminated altogether.

2. The insulation properties of wood are nearly twice as good across the grain as they are lengthwise through the end grain. In other words, a stackwall will have to be much thicker than a regular log wall to have the same rating of insulation.

3. Wood decays more readily through exposed end grain than laterally through its thickness.

4. Mortar is definitely not a good insulator. Since a typical wall will be up to 35 percent mortar, either very long blocks or insulation packed inside a space in the mortar will have to be provided.

CONSTRUCTION

There are two basic methods for putting the walls up: filling in the gaps between a post-and-beam frame, or building a free-standing block wall.

POST-AND-BEAM FRAME

The one drawback with this method is construction of the actual frame; but once you have done that, it couldn't be simpler.

The photo on this page shows a small stackwall shop that had milled 12- x 12-inch timbers used for the frame. A concrete footing was poured and angle

A beautiful double layer plank door built by the same lady seen laying blocks in the following photo.

iron plates with holes drilled in them were used to bolt the timbers to the concrete pad and also to each other. The roof trusses were bought and delivered prefabricated. Having a substantial frame such as this is helpful for a number of reasons. It gives you a solid, level plate to lay the roof trusses on, one which does not rely on the strength or the condition of the mortar to hold it up. This may prove a great advantage as the years go by. The frame also gives you reference points between which to string mason's lines, so you can keep the block wall going up plumb. It is amazing just how fast the walls

Troweling mortar onto the log blocks. Notice the mason's line that is strung between the wall timber and the door frame. This line was used to keep the wall going up straight.

This structure weathered its first season well. The major problem was that the logs, although well seasoned, shrank slightly, opening up cracks around their perimeters.

go up between the posts. Another plus is that once the roof is on, you can stack the blocks and mix the mortar inside the building out of the weather. Finally, the completion of the roof in the first summer allowed the cut blocks to be stacked under the roof for one winter. Even old barn logs will be exposed to climate changes in the process of dismantling and cutting, and should be given time to adjust.

Curing is especially important with green logs. Air drying takes two years or more to complete if the logs are stacked so that air can circulate around them. This process can be hastened by placing the logs in a small building equipped with air vents and a small wood heater for four weeks or more depending on the conditions — this functions as a drying kiln. However, it is a lot of work.

The blocks used for the building in the above photograph were cut from old cedar barn logs. They were cut to 12-inch lengths with a chain saw, a process that progressed quickly and with increasing accuracy. The first block was cut off carefully to length and used as a guide to cut the rest of them. Since it was an old barn, there was no bark to peel off, and this pleased the builders immensely. All the blocks were immersed for a minute or two in a drum of water just before being mortared into the wall. This was done so that the dry blocks would not draw too much water out of the mortar, preventing it from curing properly. There were no small round limbs used in the wall, but some of the larger round blocks were split into halves or quarters to fit in any particularly large spaces between two blocks, keeping the amount of mortar in the wall to a minimum. Half-blocks were sometimes used against the timber posts.

The rough door and window frames are 2- x 12-inch spruce. This size was chosen so they would be in proportion to the rest of the building. The rough door frames were put in place and braced level before the wood block work began and were later nailed to the blocks to make them secure. To put in the rough window frames the walls were built up almost to the height that the windows would start and then leveled with split blocks and placed flat side up, which helped level the wall off to make the frame.

The rough frame was then placed on the wall, squared and leveled, and braced in place. The block wall was then built around the frames on the sides and the top. It is easy to eye-ball the plumbness of the wall because all the materials — blocks, window, door, and post-and-beam frame — were the same 12-inch dimension. After a while, the mason's line wasn't used so much in favor of first making sure that the blocks were flush with the corner posts, and then squinting down the wall to see if it was beginning to bulge in or out.

If a wall is starting to go out of plumb, take steps to correct it right away for the obvious reason that once the mortar has hardened it's nearly impossible to change anything. A plumb bob or four-foot spirit level was not used on this particular building, but either tool would be useful. After the mortar had set, the frames were secured with six-inch spikes.

These window and door frames seemed to hold up very well with no perceivable bowing or sagging; however, you may

Built from old barn logs a number of years ago, this stackwall residence is standing up quite well. Large cracks have opened up in many of the logs and the owner has found that interior panelling is necessary. He says that once the wind leaks have been stopped the home is quite warm and easy to heat. The log blocks are 18 inches long and were cut to length at a sawmill.

Log sections will transmit airborne moisture through their length without becoming wet themselves. This ability makes Stackwall an excellent system for use in buildings to house animals as the interior will remain much dryer, as well as warmer, than buildings with stone, steel or plank walls. Dampness encourages the development and spread of sickness among animals.

want to put a lintel over the frames to ease the weight of the blocks and mortar. This can be done by putting a log lengthwise over the frames so that it extends about a foot past the opening on either side. You can split another log in half and place it behind this one to fill up any resulting space in the interior wall. The blocks were laid in horizontal rows, never more than two rows high at one time. This is so the wall won't sag under its own weight before the mortar has had a chance to set. The mortar is solid right through with no air space or insulation in the middle, because this building was made as a workshop and not a residence. The faces of the blocks were cleaned of dried mortar with a stiff wire brush and then treated with a wood preservative.

One Year Later

In this post-and-beam building, the mortar stayed white and the block faces were a honeyed brown — from a distance it looks like a giraffe's coat. Basically the building is sound, but cracks have appeared around some of the blocks even though they were cut from well-seasoned barn logs. As we have mentioned before, wood moves more than mortar. Using wood that has been drying for a hundred years only minimizes this shrinking. If some blocks were put in on a day that was damp, they

STACKWALL SHOWING CORNER DETAILS

might shrink more than blocks put in on a dry day, and so on. A log always has to be looked upon as a living thing, even one that was cut down a century ago. Even an old log that has been sitting there for a long time, will be swelling and shrinking a little with each season, and will go through more changes when cut into 12-inch lengths. Sometimes they split right through the middle, leaving a crack in the wall, from the inside to the outside, that has to be caulked. This happened to quite a few logs in this building, and the cracks between the blocks and the mortar as well as the cracks right through the blocks were patched up with caulking. Sprayed-in-place or flexible plastic foams for preventing door and window air leaks are also good solutions for drafts.

Paneling the inside of the stackwall house is relatively easy. If the wall is plumb and the block cutting precise, a frame wall to hold insulation and paneling can be easily fitted. North walls, walls exposed to direct sunlight, which will crack the most, and walls in which poorer grade materials had to be used may all qualify. When insulation is added, a vapor barrier must be applied on the warm side of the wall to prevent water from collecting in the insulating material. Adding insulation to the outside of a stackwall building is not recommended unless precautions are taken to deal with moisture migrating through from the inside. This requires either a vapor barrier on the inside surface or adequate venting of the outside insulation material.

If stucco or plaster walls are desired, these materials can be applied directly on lath which is nailed right to the blocks. No vapor barrier is needed, and moisture may be allowed to leave freely as the logs (unlike manmade insulating material) do not suffer by its presence.

As a rule you may find that adding insulation or paneling is best done on the inside of the house. This will result in a more diverse variety of interior walls for decorative purposes. The outside, however, will benefit from the casual unity and simplicity presented by the log ends.

FREE-STANDING WALL

With this method, the corners can be round, square, or any shape that you can imagine. Round corners are stronger, visually interesting and, if the arc is not too small, easy to construct. However, if you miss the security of ninety-degree corners and straight walls, simple, alternate stacking (see illustration on page 157) can be done to construct corners out of short blocks. Free-standing, or free-form, walls are constructed using standard masonry techniques. To keep the wall plumb, use a mason's line strung from temporary plumbed corner posts dug in just a bit outside the real corners. A four-foot mason's spirit level can also be used, possibly attached to a long, straight-edged board as we discussed in Chapter 3.

With a free-standing wall that has no post-and-beam frame, there is no fixed level surface on which to attach the roof. The University of Manitoba built an experimental stackwall house in which they capped all their free-standing walls with 2 x 12 Douglas fir plates, attached to the wall with anchor bolts embedded in the mortar. The roof rafters were then attached to these plates. Of course, you would have to use a little ingenuity to get these plates level. At least there is no shrinkage or settling problem as with the long log or piece-on-piece methods.

BLOCKS

The short, firewood-sized pieces of logs used for the wall are called blocks. Softwoods such as pine and cedar are the best species to use because they provide better insulation and dry faster, but you can use virtually any kind of wood. A mixture of different species of wood can be used in a wall to come up with some interesting colors and growth ring designs. Old barns or fence posts are perfect for stackwall; they are well seasoned and any rotten sections can be cut out and discarded without ruining the log as a building material. Trees that would be too small or have too much taper for other kinds of construction can be used. Old telephone poles are also excellent, as they are dry and pressure treated with preservatives, though you'll likely find them hard to come by.

Large-diameter blocks are easily used in a stackwall; they are useful because they reduce the number of pieces that will have to be handled. Smaller-sized pieces will have to be mixed into the composition, however, to minimize the amount of mortar needed in the wall.

Though it is desirable to keep the amount of mortar to a minimum for best insulation, it is important that all blocks be completely surrounded and not be allowed to touch. Consistency in this, and careful selection of appropriately sized blocks, will ensure a uniform, aesthetically pleasing house.

The bark must come off, and the logs must be dry in order to minimize the shrinkage and resulting cracks between the logs and the mortar, whichever size you use. As we have mentioned, the blocks can be 12 inches or more long. To cut them to length, you can use a chain saw and tape measure or just cut free hand. This method is understandably very quick and not very accurate unless you use a jig of some kind, or just get the feel of it after some practice. At any rate, you are building a relatively rough wall so it's not too critical. Another way is to use a large circular saw with a cradle for the log to sit in and a stop installed so that the logs can be quickly cut.

MORTAR

Because the mortar comprises such a large proportion of the wall, it becomes a very important component and must be mixed and applied accordingly. It should be pliable enough so that it can be easily worked. This is why plasticisers such as hydrated lime are used in the mix. It also must be strong enough and stiff enough to hold up the blocks in the wall without sagging or flowing — these qualities are controlled by the amount of water in the mix, and the proportions of cement and lime to sand. The mortar is composed of brick sand, cement and lime mixed in the proportions listed in the appendix.

To improve the plasticity and the adhesion of the mortar, the lime used should be "slaked" by sifting it into a barrel of water and leaving it to stand at least 24 hours, much longer if possible. The idea is to thoroughly saturate the lime which is slow to absorb water. Slaked lime is added to the mix after the dry ingredients have been mixed and enough water has been added to make it begin to "ball up." When the lime has been mixed in, add more water if necessary to get a good workable consistency. Slaked lime makes the mortar much less likely to slump and run off.

The sand can be cleaned by fitting a screen over a wooden frame, propping it up on an angle and throwing shovelfuls of the sand through it to get out the coarser stone; or clean brick sand can be bought from a commercial supplier. The water used should be clean as well. The proportion of water to mix is up to the person who is doing the mixing, something that you will catch on to faster than you might think. Just remember to add the water a little at a time because it does have a tendency to thin out rapidly, and it's not a good idea to add more dry aggregate to thicken it.

Always mix the dry aggregate before adding the water.

The mortar is worked in with a large triangular-shaped mason's trowel and smoothed off with a smaller one. You should always wear gloves because the sand and lime are very abrasive to finger tips and cement has a nasty habit of drying out the skin. Make sure that you keep the wet mix out of the direct sunlight so that it doesn't dry before you have a chance to use it.

BUILDING FOR WARMTH

Here are three basic stackwall methods:

Simple Log and Mortar

This method was used in the post-and-beam building shown in the photo on page 153. The mortar's high thermal conductivity is compensated for by the formidable strength of the finished wall. For barns and outbuildings, blocks as short as eight inches will provide a warm, damp-free environment.

Lengthening the blocks increases their R-value and strength proportionally. Using blocks up to thirty inches long will produce both the strength needed for above-grade (above-ground) barn foundations and the insulation required for a house in the coldest of climates.

Log with Insulated Mortar

In this type of wall, the blocks are supported with a four-inch bead of mortar on the inside and outside edges. The space in the middle is filled with insulation. Any type of insulation will do: foam, fiberglass, wood chips mixed with lime (lime discourages insects and rodents), or even just a dead air space. Ground-up scrap styrofoam is a good choice as it has a high R-factor and doesn't tend to settle over time.

Double Wall with Insulation Sandwich

This method is about as complicated as any practical stackwall construction might be, but is certainly the warmest way to go. Instead of single rows of logs, this method employs a double row of shorter logs with a space in the middle between the rows. The walls are tied together by logs which span the full width of the two walls every three or four feet. The space between the rows is filled with insulation. Using a solid sheet of foam insulation between the logs would stop drafts of air which may come through cracks in the exterior part of the wall.

The owner of the stackwall workshop in the photo on page 153, has applied his engineering knowledge to reach comparative R-factors for different types and thicknesses of walls. The results are based on the use of eastern white cedar blocks and a finished wall surface that is seventy percent wood and thirty percent mortar.

A 12-inch-thick wall, with blocks

embedded in solid mortar has an R-factor of 5.3.

A 24-inch-thick wall incorporating a 16-inch cavity in the centre of the masonry, and packed with wood chips and lime, produces an R-value of 18.3.

A double wall sandwiched with two 12-inch blocks spaced eight inches apart, and packed with wood shavings, will increase the R-factor to 21.8.

It's interesting to note that the time and energy devoted to constructing a double wall only marginally increases its insulating value. This is in spite of the fact that its overall thickness is eight inches greater than the two-foot-thick hollow wall discussed earlier. Further drawbacks of the double wall include: the need for a larger amount of mortar — 24 inches thick, as opposed to eight inches for the hollow wall — and the difficulty of fitting tie blocks to hold together two separate and independent walls as they go up simultaneously.

Combining methods, as in the use of an 18-inch hollow wall with an inside addition of R-12 insulation (four-inch fiberglass batts) to produce an R-factor of 26, may be the most effective course where climate demands.

INSULATION VALUES FOR STACKWALL CONSTRUCTION

Type	Insulation	Thickness wood	Thickness Insulation	R-factor	
Simple log and mortar	none	1 foot	0	5.3	
Log with insulated mortar	wood shavings	2 foot	1 foot, 4 inches	18.3	
Double wall with insulation sandwich	wood shavings	1 foot & 1 foot	8 inches	21.8	This figure will be greater if styrofoam is used.
Square pine timber. Rated across grains	0	1 foot	0	10.4	(With 10 percent of area being uninsulated mortar)

aPPenDix

PRESERVATIVES

1. ANTISTAIN SOLUTION FOR FRESHLY-PEELED LOGS

Mix 1 to 3 pounds of sodium pentachlorophenate with 12 gallons (approximately 100 pounds) of water. Brush solution on logs within one day of peeling, especially in warm weather.

2. WATER REPELLANT PRESERVATIVE

Ingredients	For 1 gallon	For 5 gallons
40% pentachlorophenol (10:1 concentrate)	1¾ cups	2 quarts
Boiled linseed oil	1½ cups	1¾ quarts
Paraffin wax	1 ounce	4-5 ounces
Solvent (mineral spirits, Paint thinner or turpentine)	Add to make 1 gallon	Add to make 5 gallons

Melt the paraffin in a container heated with hot water. Be sure the solvent is at room temperature. Slowly pour the hot paraffin into the solvent mixing the new combination vigorously to keep the wax from solidifying at the bottom of the container. Add the linseed oil and the pentachlorophenol. Stir until the mixture is uniform.

Brush the mixture into cracks or joints.

If the solution is held at low temperature it may separate. If this occurs, raise the mixture to room temperature and stir.

3. NATURAL FINISH (PIGMENTED) PRESERVATIVE

For exterior surfaces of the finished log cabin, for decay resistance and color, the pigmented natural finish provides a durable, relatively inexpensive treatment. The following solution should be applied at the rate of about 150 square feet per gallon.

Ingredients for approximately 5 gallons	Quantity
40 percent pentachlorophenol (10:1 concentrate)	2 quarts
Boiled linseed oil	3 gallons
Paraffin wax	1 pound
Solvent (mineral spirits, turpentine, or paint thinner)	1 gallon
Tinting colors (according to list below)	1 to 2 quarts
Zinc stearate	1 cup
If available, can be added to reduce the tendency of the pigment to cake during storage.	

Some suggested colors are:

Desired color	Pigment(s) required	Pigment quantities for 5 gallons of stain
Cedar	Burnt sienna	1 pint
	Raw umber	+1 pint
Light redwood	Burnt sienna	1 quart
Chocolate brown	Burnt umber	1 quart
Fruitwood brown	Raw sienna	1 pint
	Raw umber	+1 pint
	Burnt sienna	+1/2 pint
Tan	Raw sienna	1 quart
	Burnt umber	+3 fluid ounces
Green gold	Chrome oxide	1 pint
	Raw sienna	+1 pint
Forest green	Medium chrome green	1 quart
Smoky gray	White house paint	1 quart
	Raw umber	+6 fluid ounces
	Lamp black	+3 fluid ounces

These are available from hardware stores.

Pigmented stains are the most durable when applied to rough or weathered surfaces. When two coats are applied to a rough surface, the second coat should be applied before the first has dried so that both coats can penetrate. Stain that remains on the surface after 3 or 4 hours should be wiped up or rubbed in to provide a uniform flat appearance. To avoid lap marks in the application of penetrating stain, the full length of a log should be finished without stopping for more than 5 minutes. The finish should also be stirred frequently to maintain uniform suspension of the pigments.

(Reprinted from *Protecting Log Cabins from Decay*, by W. C. Feist, research chemist, Forest Products Laboratory, Forest Service, U.S. Department of Agriculture.)

Note: Amounts of preservative necessary should be carefully calculated. It is better to have to mix another small batch than to have to dispose of leftovers. (Amounts given are for U.S. gallons.)

MORTAR MIXES

1. FOR REGULAR CHINKING

    2 parts Portland cement
    1 part dry hydrated lime
    6 parts clean sharp brick sand.

A commercially available mortar plasticizer may be substituted for the lime. Under some conditions it will improve workability while at the same time reducing whiteness.

2. FOR WHITER CHINKING

In place of regular Portland, substitute a commercially available special white mortar or "stone set." Plasticizers and lime tend to weaken cement. Their amounts should be regulated so that you produce a somewhat low strength and soft chinking. A high strength mix tends to be too brittle and prone to cracking, but too much lime will weaken the cement and cause it to crumble. (This is a mix which has been recommended to us by the Ontario Agricultural Museum.)

    2 parts white stone set
    1 part plasticizer
    6 parts clean sharp sand

3. FOR STACKWALL CONSTRUCTION

A. Recommended by the University of Manitoba.

    1 part Portland cement
    $1/2$ part hydrated lime
    4 parts clean, sharp sand.

This makes a good, stiff (but workable) mix for stackwall construction without a main frame.

B. Recommended by Armstrong, Vanderstaal and Zadra. Use the same formula as above, with the exception that the lime is slaked before use (see method for slaking on page 159).

INSULATION VALUES

Building Material	Thickness in Inches	R-value
Insultating fiberboard	1	2.38
Insulating sheathing	$5/8$	1.49
Insulating sheathing	$1/2$	1.19
Plywood	1	1.25
Gypsum board (drywall	$1/2$	0.63
Hardwood	1	0.91
Softwood	1	1.25
Western cedar	1	1.56
Loose fill insulation		
Cellulose fiber	1	3.57 to 4
Mineral fibers		
(2 to 5 pounds density)	1	2.5 to 3.33
Vermiculite		
(expanded mica		
7 pounds density)	1	2.08 to 2.5
Batt-type insulation	2-$2^1/2$	7
(Fiberglass or rock	3-$3^1/2$	10
wool)	6	20
Expanded polystyrene		3.45 to 4
(beadboard)	1	
Styrofoam	1	5
Polyurethane	1	5.88 to 6
Air space	$3/4$ to 4	0.97
Brick (clay or shale)	4	0.42 to 0.44
Concrete block	4	0.71
(3 oval core, sand and	8	1.11
gravel composition)	12	1.28
Cinder block	4	1.11
	8	1.72
	12	1.89
Inside air film resistance		0.68
Outside air film resistance		0.17

Reprinted from *100 Ways to Save Energy and Money in the Home*, published by the Department of Energy Mines and Resources Canada, Ottawa.

Note: 'R' means resistance to heat transference. R-values may be added together.

MINIMUM SIZES AND CLEARANCES IN HOUSE DESIGN

1. BATHROOM (three piece)

Room size: Minimum 40 square feet with smallest dimension no less than 5 feet.

Fixture clearances: (minimum spaces, in inches, required for fixtures):

	Width of space	Depth of fixture	Front clearance	Total depth of space
Sink	28	25	18	43
Toilet	30	16	18	34
Tub	60	32	20	53
Shower	36	36	18	54

2. KITCHEN

Entry door minimum: 32 inches
Entry hall minimum: 36 inches
Room size minimum: 50 square feet, with no dimension less than 7 feet (kitchenette)
Minimum distance between counters: 36 inches
Minimum distance between counter and wall: 36 inches
Normal depth of counter top: 24 inches
Fridge: average width 30 inches, depth 28 inches
Stove: average width 30 inches, depth 28 inches
Sink (double): average width 32 inches, depth 20 inches.

3. CLOSETS

Minimum depth, inside measure: 22 inches
Minimum width, inside measure: 30 inches

4. DINING ROOM

Should have no dimension less than 10 feet.
Minimum clearances for table and chairs arrangement:
Table edge to wall: 30 inches (with chair between)
Table width: 30 inches (people seated both sides)
Total clearance for table with chairs to both sides: 90 inches

5. HALLWAY

Minimum 36 inches (plus allowance for stairwell railing, if any)

6. STAIR DIMENSIONS

Maximum rise: 8 inches
Minimum run: $8^1/_4$ inches
Minimum tread width: $9^1/_4$ inches
Minimum overall width: 2 feet, 10 inches
Minimum head clearance (measured vertically from a line drawn through the outer edges of the nosing) 6 feet, 4 inches.

7. MINIMUM ROOF PITCH

Asphalt shingles — normal application: 4/12
Asphalt shingles — low slope application: 2/12
Roll roofing: 2/12
Wood shingles: 3/12
Handsplit shakes: 4/12

Note: In calculating minimum roof pitch, the fractions used above give two numbers. The first number represents the roof rise, which is the distance from the wall plate to the roof peak. The second number, which is always 12, represents the roof run, which is half the width of the building, or the horizontal distance between the roof peak and the outside face of the wall plate.

Glossary

Aggregate. Coarse material, such as gravel, broken stone or sand, with which cement and water are mixed to form concrete. Crushed stone is usually designated as coarse aggregate and sand as fine aggregate.

Airway. The space left between roof insulation and roof decking to allow free movement of air.

Anchor Bolt. A steel bolt used to secure a structural member against uplift. It is usually deformed at one end to ensure a good grip in the concrete or masonry in which it is embedded.

Angle Iron. An L-shaped steel section frequently used to support masonry over a window or door opening.

Apron. A plain or molded finish piece below the stool of a window, installed to cover the rough edge of the wall finish. Also an extension of the concrete floor of a garage or other structure beyond the face of the building.

Asbestos Cement. A fire-resisting weather-proof building material, made from Portland Cement and asbestos. It is manufactured in various forms such as plain sheets, corrugated sheets, shingles, pipes, etc.

Attic or Roof Space. The space between the top floor ceiling and roof and between a dwarf partition and sloping roof.

Back Fill. The material used to refill an excavation around the outside of a foundation wall or pipe trench.

Balloon Framing. A method of wood-frame construction in which the studs extend in one piece from the foundation sill to the top plate supporting the roof.

Baseboard. A molded board placed against the wall around a room next to the floor to conceal the joint between the floor and wall finish.

Base Course. In masonry the first or bottom course of brick or masonry blocks.

Batten. A narrow strip of wood used to cover joints between boards or panels. Board and batten is the term used to describe the type of cladding for wood frame buildings in which battens cover the joints between boards.

Batter Board. Boards set at right angles to each other at each corner of an excavation, used to indicate the level and alignment of the foundation wall.

Bay Window. Window which projects outside the main line of a building.

Beam. A horizontal structural member usually wood, steel or concrete used to support vertical loads.

Beam Pocket. A notch formed at the top of a foundation wall to receive and support the end of a beam.

Bearing. The part of a joist, rafter, truss or beam which actually rests on its support and the area of support on which it rests.

Bearing Wall. A wall that supports any vertical load in addition to its own weight.

Bed. In masonry, the horizontal layer of mortar on which each course of masonry is laid. Generally any horizontal surface which has been prepared to receive the element(s) it will support.

Bevel. The sloping surface formed when two surfaces meet at an angle which is not a right angle.

Bevel Siding. Boards tapered to a thin edge and used as exterior wall covering.

Blind-Nailing. Nailing in such a way that the nailheads are not finally visible on the face of the work.

Bond. In masonry, the pattern in which bricks or blocks are laid to tie the individual units together so that the entire wall they comprise will tend to act as a complete unit.

Bottom Plate. The lower horizontal member of a wood-frame wall nailed to the bottom of the wall studs and to the floor framing members.

Bracing or Cross Bracing. Diagonal framing members used to brace a frame wall for the application of vertical siding which provides no lateral support. Not necessary when using plywood or diagonal board underlay. Bracing is cut into large dimension studs and nailed between smaller dimension studs.

Breaking Joints. The manner of laying masonry units so as to avoid vertical joints in adjacent courses from lining up. Also the distribution of joints in boards, flooring, lath and panels so no two adjacent end-joints are directly in line.

Brick Veneer. A facing of brick tied to a wood-frame or masonry wall, serving as a wall covering only and carrying no structural loads.

Bridging (Cross). Small wood or metal members that are inserted in a diagonal position between adjacent floor or roof joists.

Buck Plate. A vertical structural member, usually of two-inch material, which is nailed to the ends of log sections at window and door openings to secure them in place and to each other, and to which the window or door unit is nailed.

Built-up Roof. A roof covering composed of three or more layers of roofing felt or fiberglass saturated with coal tar or asphalt. The top is finished with crushed stone, gravel or a cap sheet. Generally used on flat or low-pitched roofs.

Butt-Joint. Any joint made by fastening two members together without overlapping.

Cant Hook. A device used to roll heavy logs.

Come-Along. A lever-operated device used to move heavy objects.

Common Rafter. One of a series of rafters extending from the top of an exterior wall to the ridge of a roof.

Corner Bead. In plastering, a metal strip placed on external corners before plastering to protect, align and reinforce them. In gypsum board finish, a strip of metal or wood fixed to external corners to protect them from damage.

Corner Boards. A built-up wood member installed vertically on the external corners of a house or other frame structure against which the ends of the siding are butted.

Cornerite. Metal lath cut into strips and bent to a right angle. Used in internal angles of plastered walls and ceilings as reinforcing.

Counterflashing. A flashing applied above another flashing to shed water over the top of the under flashing and to allow some differential movement without damage to the flashing.

Course. A continuous layer of bricks or masonry units in buildings; the term is also applicable to shingles.

Crawl Space. A shallow space between the lowest floor of a house and the ground beneath.

Cricket. A small roof structure at the junction of a chimney and a roof to divert rain water around the chimney.

Cant Strip. A wedge or triangular-shaped piece of lumber generally installed in the deck of a flat roof around the perimeter or at the junction of the roof and an adjoining wall.

Casing. A form of molded trim used around window and door openings.

Ceramic Tiles. Vitreous clay tile used for a surface finish.

Chimney Flue. A passage housed in a chimney through which smoke and gases are carried from a fuel-burning appliance, fireplace or incinerator to the exterior.

Chinking. The material used to fill the gap between the logs in the walls of log buildings. Refers to the process of filling the gaps as well as the material used.

Collar Brace. A horizontal piece of lumber used to provide intermediate support for opposite roof rafters, usually located in the middle third of the rafters. Also called collar beam or collar tie.

Colombage. A method of construction, French in origin, similar to the English "half-timber" style, in which the spaces between the timbers are filled with brickwork and plaster. Also *colombage pierroté* where the spaces are filled with stonework.

Cross Tie Log. Horizontal structural members which span a building to connect opposite walls at their tops and prevent them from bulging outward.

Curing (of Concrete). The maintenance of proper temperature and moisture conditions to promote the continued chemical reaction which takes place between the water and the cement.

Dado. A rectangular groove in a board or plank. In interior decoration, a special type of wall treatment.

Damp-Proof Course. A damp-proof material placed just above the ground level in a brick or stone wall to prevent ground moisture from seeping up through the structure.

Damp-Proofing. The process of coating the outside of a foundation wall with a special preparation to resist passage of moisture through the wall. Material used to resist the passage of moisture through concrete floor slabs and from masonry to wood.

Double Glazing. Two panes of glass in a door or window, with an air space between the panes. They may be sealed hermetically as a single unit or each pane may be installed separately in the door or window sash.

Drywall Finish. Interior wall and ceiling finish other than plaster — e.g., gypsum board, plywood, fiberboard panels, etc.

Dwarf Wall. A framed wall of less than normal full height.

Eave. The lower part of a roof which projects beyond the face of the walls.

Eave Soffit. The under surface of the eave.

Eaves Trough. A trough fixed to an eave to collect and carry away the run-off from the roof. Also called a gutter.

Edge Grain. Lumber that is sawn along the radius of the annual rings or at an angle less than 45 degrees to the radius is edge-grained; this term is synonymous with quarter-sawn.

End Grain. The face of a piece of lumber which is exposed when the fibers are cut transversely.

End Matched. Having tongue-and-groove ends.

Expanded Metal. A metal network formed by stamping or cutting sheet-metal and stretching it to form open meshes. It is used as reinforcing in concrete construction and as lath for plastering and stucco.

Expansion Joint. A joint in a concrete or masonry structure designed to permit expansion without damage to the structure.

Face Nailing. Fastening a member by driving nails through it at right angles to its exposed surface.

Fascia Board. A finish member around the face of eaves and roof projections.

Feathering. Reducing gradually to a very thin edge.

Filler Logs.　　Those short portions of log which run between two openings in the same wall and are supported by buck plates rather than by interlocking at the corners of a building. Also: the logs which fill the sections between the vertical structural timbers in the piece-on-piece construction method.

Fire Clay.　　A clay of high heat-resisting qualities used to make fire brick and the mortar in which fire brick is laid.

Fire Stop.　　A complete obstruction placed across a concealed air space in a wall, floor or roof to retard or prevent the spread of flame and hot gases.

Flange.　　A projecting edge, rib or rim; the top and bottom of I-beams and channels are called flanges.

Flashing.　　Sheet metal or other material used in roof and wall construction to shed water.

Flooring.　　Material used in the construction of floors. The surface material is known as finish flooring while the base material is called subflooring.

Flue.　　See Chimney Flue.

Flue Lining.　　The material (usually tile pipe in 2-foot lengths) which lines the flue to protect the chimney walls from hot gases.

Footing.　　The widened section, usually concrete, at the base or bottom of a foundation wall, pier, or column.

Foundation.　　The lower portion, usually concrete or masonry and including the footings, which transfers the weight of, and loads on, a building to the ground.

Furring.　　Strips of wood applied to a wall or other surface as nailing support for the finish material, or to give the wall an appearance of greater thickness.

Gable.　　The upper triangular-shaped portion of the end wall of a house.

Gable End.　　The entire end wall of a house having a gable roof.

Gauge.　　A standard for measuring, e.g. diameter of nails or wire and thickness of metal sheets, etc.

Grade (Lumber).　　To separate lumber into different established classifications depending upon its suitability for different uses. A classification of lumber.

Grade.　　The surface slope. The level of the ground surface around the foundation wall. To modify the ground surface by cut and fill.

Grade Line.　　A predetermined line indicating the proposed elevation of the ground surface around a building.

Grounds.　　Strips of wood that are attached to walls before plastering along the floor line and around windows, doors and other openings as a plaster stop and thickness guide.

Grout.　　A thin mixture of cement mortar and additional water.

Header (Framing).　　A wood member at right angles to a series of joists or rafters at which the joists or rafters terminate. When used at openings in the floor or roof system the header supports the joist or rafters and acts as a beam.

Hearth.　　The floor of the fireplace and immediately in front.

Hip.　　The sloping ridge of a roof formed by two intersecting roof slopes.

Hip-Rafter.　　The rafter which forms the hip of a roof.

I-Beam.　　A steel beam with a cross section resembling the letter "I."

Insulation.　　Material used to resist heat transmission through walls, floors and roofs.

Interior Finish.　　The covering used on interior walls and ceilings.

Jack Rafter.　　A short rafter that spans from the wallplate to a hip rafter or from a valley rafter to the roof ridge.

Jamb.　　The side post or lining of a doorway, window, or other opening.

Joint Cement.　　A powder which is mixed with water and applied to the joints between sheets of gypsum-wallboard.

Joist.　　One of a series of horizontal wood members, usually two-inch nominal thickness, used to support a floor, ceiling or roof.

Joist Hanger.　　A steel section shaped like a stirrup, bent so it can be fastened to a beam to provide end support for joists, headers, etc.

Kerf.　　The groove formed in wood by a saw cut.

King Post.　　A vertical structural member used to transfer the weight of the ridge beam onto the gable end walls or onto horizontal cross beams.

Lath.　　A building element made of wood, metal, gypsum, or fiberboard fastened to the frame of a building to serve as a plaster base.

Ledger Strip.　　A strip of lumber fastened along the bottom of the side of a beam on which joists rest.

Lintel.　　A horizontal structural member (beam) that supports the load over an opening such as a door or window.

Log Dog.　　A steel bar with spikes on both ends which is driven into a log to hold it still while it is being worked on.

Log Tongs.　　Pointed tongs used to grip logs for hauling and lifting. As the force of pulling is exerted, the gripping points of the tongs are automatically forced tighter into the log being pulled.

Long Log. A style of building employing round logs in which the full log lengths which form each wall are interlocked at their corners. Each log is grooved out on its underside to fit tightly over the log below and prevent air and water from passing between them.

Lookout Rafters. Short wood members cantilevered over a wall to support an overhanging portion of a roof.

Louver. A slatted opening for ventilation in which the slats are so placed to exclude rain, sunlight, or vision.

Mesh. Expanded metal or woven wire used as a reinforcement for concrete, plaster or stucco.

Metal Lath. Expanded metal or woven wire used to provide a base for plaster or stucco.

Mineral Wool. A material used for insulating buildings, produced by sending a blast of steam through molten slag or rock, common types now in use include rock wool, glass wool and slag wool.

Miter Joint. A joint formed by cutting and butting two pieces of board on a line bisecting the angle of their junction.

Mortar. A substance produced from prescribed proportions of cementing agents, aggregates and water which gradually sets hard after mixing.

Mortar Bed. Layer of mortar on which any structural member, masonry unit or tile is bedded.

Mudsill. Timber placed directly on the ground as a foundation for a structure.

Newel. A post to which the end of a stair railing or balustrade is fastened. Also, any post to which a railing or balustrade is fastened.

Non-Bearing Partition. A wall which separates space into rooms, but supports no vertical load except its own weight.

Nosing. The rounded and projecting edge of a stair tread, window sill, etc.

O.G. or Ogee. A molding with a profile in the form of a letter S; having the outline of a reversed curve.

On Center. A term used to define the point from which measurements are taken — from the center of one member to the center of the adjacent member as in the spacing of studs, joists or nails. Also center to center.

Panel. A large, thick board or sheet of lumber, plywood, or other material. A thin board with all its edges inserted in a groove of a surrounding frame of thick material. A portion of a flat surface recessed or sunk below the surrounding area, distinctly set off by molding or some other decorative device. Also, a section of floor, wall, ceiling, or roof, usually prefabricated and of large size, handled as a single unit in the operations of assembly and erection.

Parapet Wall. That part of an exterior, party or firewall extending above the roof line; a wall which serves as a guard at the edge of a balcony or roof.

Parging. A coat of plaster or cement mortar applied to masonry or concrete walls.

Piece-on-Piece. A style of building in which short lengths of log are used to form wall panels in sections between vertical support beams which form the main structural frame of a building. Also known as *pièce-en-pièce* and *pièces-sur-pièces*.

Pier. A column of masonry, usually rectangular in horizontal cross section, used to support other structural members.

Pilaster. A pier forming an integral part of a wall and partially projecting from the wall face.

Pitch. Also "slope." Inclination to the horizontal plane.

Pitched Roof. A roof which has one or more surfaces sloping at angles greater than necessary for drainage.

Plain Concrete. Unreinforced concrete.

Plough. To cut a groove.

Plumb. Vertical. To make vertical.

Plumbing. The pipes, fixtures and other apparatus for the water supply and the removal of water-borne wastes.

Purlin. A horizontal structural member used to support roof rafters at some point between the wall plate and ridge beam.

Queen Post. A vertical structural member used to transfer the weight of roof purlins onto the gable ends or onto horizontal cross beams.

Rabbet. A groove cut in the surface along the edge of a board, plank, or other timber. The recess in a brick jamb which receives a window frame. Also the recess in a door frame to receive the door.

Radiant Heating. A method of heating, usually consisting of coils or pipes, or electric heating elements placed in the floor, wall, or ceiling.

Rafter. One of the series of structural members of a roof usually of two-inch nominal thickness designed to support roof loads, but not ceiling finish.

Receptacle (Electric). A wall-mounted electrical outlet.

Ribbon. A narrow board let into studs to support joists.

Ridge Beam. A horizontal structural member usually two inches thick, supporting the upper ends of the rafters.

Ridge Board. A horizontal member usually $3/4$-inch thick at the upper end of the rafters, to which these rafters are nailed.

Scratch Coat. The first coat of plaster, which is scratched to form a bond for the second coat.

Scribing. Fitting woodwork to an irregular surface. A term used in long log building to refer to the process of transferring the contours of one log onto another log so that they may be cut to fit tightly together.

Sealer. A liquid applied directly over uncoated wood for the purpose of sealing the surface.

Shake. A shingle split (not sawn) from a block of wood and used for roofing and siding.

Sheathing Paper. Paper treated with tar or asphalt used under exterior wall cladding as protection against the passage of water or air.

Shed Roof. A sloping roof having its surface in one plane.

Shoe Mold. For interior finish, a molding strip placed against the baseboard at the floor; also called base shoe, or carpet strip.

Siding. In wood-frame construction, the material other than masonry or stucco used as an exterior wall covering.

Sill. The horizontal member forming the bottom of an opening such as a door or window.

Sill Plate. A structural member anchored to the top of a foundation wall, upon which the floor joists rest.

Sleepers. Round poles with one flattened side which lay on the ground or are notched into the first round of logs and to which the floor boards are nailed. An old word used to describe floor joists in a primitive cabin without foundations.

Smoke Pipe. A pipe conveying products of combustion from a solid or liquid fuel-fired appliance to a chimney flue.

Socket Slick. A large tool shaped like a chisel usually longer than 18 inches with a blade width of three inches, which is pushed by hand rather than driven by a hammer. Used in making timber joints, corner joints and generally in shaping beams.

Soffit. The underside of elements of a building, such as staircases, roof overhangs, beams, etc.

Sole Plate. The lower horizontal member of a wood frame wall nailed to the bottom of the wall studs and to the floor framing members. Also called a bottom plate.

Span. The horizontal distance between supports for beams, joists, rafters, etc.

Splash Block. A small masonry block laid with the top close to the ground surface to receive roof drainage and divert it away from the building.

Stackwall. A style of log building in which logs of one to three feet in length are laid in a bed of mortar with their end grain exposed, enough of such logs being laid to form the desired walls of the building. Also called cord wood construction.

Stair Landing. A platform between flights of stairs.

Starter log. The first logs laid down on the foundation when beginning a house, usually on its longest side.

Step Flashing. Rectangular or square pieces of flashing used at the junction of shingled roof and walls. Also called shingle flashing.

Stool. The flat, narrow shelf forming the top member of the interior trim at the bottom of a window.

Stoop. A low platform with or without steps, outside the entrance door of a house.

Storm Door. An extra outside door for protection gainst inclement weather.

Strike Plate. The part of a door lock set which is fastened to the jamb.

Strut. A structural member which is designed to resist longitudinal compressive stress such as members supporting a ridge beam or rafters; a short column.

Stud. One of a series of wood structural members (usually two-inch nominal thickness) used as supporting elements in walls and partitions. (Plural: Studs or studding.)

Subfloor. Boards or sheet material laid on joists under a finish floor.

Taping. In dry-wall construction the masking of joints between sheets by means of paper tape which is smoothed over with joint cement.

Three-Way Switch. A switch used in house wiring when a light (or lights) is controlled from two places. A three-way switch must be used at each location.

Threshold. A strip of wood, metal, or other material bevelled on each edge and used at the junction of two different floor finishes under doors, or on top of the door sill at exterior doors.

Toenailing. Nailing at an angle to the first member so as to ensure penetration into a second member.

Tongue-and-Groove Lumber. Any lumber, such as boards or planks, machined in such a manner that there is a groove on one edge and a corresponding tongue on the other.

Top Plate. In building, the horizontal member nailed to the top of the partition or wall studs.

Tread. The horizontal part of a step.

Trimmer. A beam or joist alongside an opening and into which a header is framed.

V-Groove. A term used in long log building to refer to the part of the underside of a log which has been cut out to fit over the log below in styles not requiring chinking.

Valley. The internal angle formed by the junction of two sloping sides of a roof.

Valley Rafters. Rafters which are located at the center of roof valleys to support the jack rafters.

Vapor Barrier. Material used to retard the passage of water vapor or moisture.

Wall Plates. In wood-frame construction, the horizontal members attached to the ends of the studs. Also called top or bottom plates, depending on their location.

Water Table. The level below which the ground is saturated with water.

Weatherstripping. Strips of felt, rubber, metal or other material, fixed along the edges of doors or windows to keep out drafts and reduce heat loss.

Weephole. A small hole, as at the bottom of a retaining wall or masonry veneer, to drain water to the exposed face.

Wythe. A continuous vertical section of a masonry wall having a thickness of one masonry unit.

Note: This glossary has been adapted from the one found in *Canadian Wood-Frame House Construction*, and is used with the permission of Central Mortgage and Housing Corporation, Ottawa.

We offer the following selection of books which fall into two categories: first, those we have used in our research for this book; and second, those we believe readers will find useful in learning more about log building in particular, and building and architecture in general.

Arcand, R. D. *Log Building Tools and How to Use Them.* Sorrinto, B.C.: R–J, 1976. The only book available that deals exclusively with log building tools. Since a lot of these tools exist only as collectors' items, this goes a long way toward correcting the problem. It not only shows what you will need (in some cases tools you might never have heard of), but also how to make them. A must for the serious log builder.

Architecture in Wood: A History of Wood Building Techniques in Europe and North America. Hans Jurgen Hanson (Ed.). London: Faber and Faber, 1971. An excellent book, with beautiful photographs; for anyone interested in the architecture of building with wood over the years. Some spectacular examples of early buildings.

Blackburn, Graham. *Illustrated Basic Carpentry.* New York: Bobbs-Merrill, 1976. The notes of a first-time house-builder, giving helpful advice on his house-in-progress, hints not often thought of by professional builders.

Brandon, Raphael and J. Arthur. *Open Timber Roofs of the Middle Ages.* Prince George, B.C.: The Canadian Log House, 1977. Spectacular examples of timber framing in medieval churches and cathedrals.

Bruyere, Christian. *In Harmony with Nature.* New York: Drake Publishing, 1975. This book and the following one are two good books about living in the country; they include information on house design, space, heat and light, and a lot of information about log building.

Bruyere, Christian and Robert Inwood (Ed.). *Country Comforts.* New York: Drake Publishing, 1975.

Canadian Wood-Frame House Construction. Ottawa, Ont.: Central Mortgage and Housing Corp. Well illustrated and easy to understand, this book covers most basic aspects of standard house construction.

Carpenters and Builders Library. Indianapolis, Indiana: Theodore Audel & Co., 1977. A series of books about carpentry and building for those who are serious about learning about the subject. Titles include *Tools, Steel Square, Joinery, Layouts, Foundations, Framing* and *Builders Math, Plans, Specifications.*

Clemson, Donovan. *Living with Logs: British Columbia's Log Buildings and Rail Fences.* Saanichton, B.C.: Hancock House, 1974. A history of the log buildings on Canada's west coast, and a look at the lifestyle of the people who have lived in them. Abundantly illustrated with photographs of abandoned houses, disintegrating shake roofs, as well as well-kept buildings and their owners. Includes a chapter on rail fences and an excellent chapter on Scandinavian-style log houses of British Columbia.

The Penguin Dictionary of Architecture. John Fleming, Hugh Honour and Nikolaus Pevsner (Ed.). New York: Penguin Books, 1973. Focuses primarily on historical aspects of architecture, rather than on detailed practical information.

Downing, A. J. *The Architecture of Country Houses.* London: Dover Publications, 1979. Originally published in 1850, this is a book about the design of nineteenth-century country houses. Mr. Downing is recognized as one of North America's first great architects; he introduced some interesting, low-cost features to the homes of the middle class that had previously only been found in mansions. The English country house is used as the basic model. This is an important book on American culture and Victorian architecture.

Elliott, Stuart and Eugenie Wallas. *The Timber Framing Book.* Maine: Housesmiths Press, 1977. This book does a good job of saving the old knowledge of timber framing, another example of a skill that has almost died out with the old-timers who have possessed it. A good historical treatment as well as the practical side of this huge subject.

The Fox Fire Book No. 1. Eliot Wigginton (Ed.). Garden City, N. Y.: Doubleday & Company, Inc., 1972. The first volume in this well-known series of books in which are collected the folklore of the Appalachians contains some useful information on log building, as well as on tools, wood, making your own shingles, and a taste of the historical climate in which log buildings have developed.

DiDonno, Lupe and Phyllis Sperling. *How to Design and Build Your Own House.* New York: Alfred A. Knopf, 1978. An aesthetic and practical approach to design; beautifully illustrated, with good photographs. Covers many aspects from site selection to functional planning to interior finishing.

Grillo, Paul Jacques. *Form, Function and Design.* London: Dover Publications, 1960. An exploration of what makes good design. Covers topics such as natural curves, interaction of textures and materials, integration with landscape. More aesthetic than practical.

Henstridge, Jack. *Building the Cordwood Home.* Oromocto, N.B.: 1978. This is a small book telling of one man's experience in building a cordwood (stackwall) home. Although we would not recommend all of the author's methods, the book could be useful for those interested in learning more about this method.

Kennedy, Clyde C. *The Upper Ottawa Valley.* Pembroke, Ont.: Renfrew County Council, 1970. Focuses on the geography, history and culture of Ontario's Ottawa Valley.

Kirchner, Harold B. *Wiring Installation and Maintenance.* Toronto: McGraw-Hill Ryerson, 1978. A clear do-it-yourself approach to wiring for the non-professional.

Lawson, Harold. *Le Chateau Montebello . . . as It Was in the Beginning.* Montreal: Canadian Pacific.

Mackie, B. Allan. *Building with Logs.* Prince George, B.C.: The Canadian Log House, (sixth edition) 1977. The well-known book about building long log homes (as opposed to cabins), with Mackie's personal opinions about everything from log building to lifestyles.

Mackie, B. Allan. *Notches of All Kinds: A Book of Timber Joinery.* Prince George, B.C.: The Canadian Log House, 1977. A unique, step-by-step book on the notches used in log building. Useful if you want to do timber framing or learn some of the more exotic notches. A good chapter on tools.

McRaven, Charles. *Building the Hewn Log House.* Hollister, Missouri: Mountain Publishing Services, 1978. A well-written book about reconstructing hewn log houses, by someone who obviously loves working with logs. A good feeling for the history of the Ozark Mountain area where the author works.

One Hundred Ways to Save Energy and Money in the Home. Ottawa, Ont.: Energy, Mines and Resources Canada. Helpful information about insulating and re-insulating for everyone to understand.

Peters, John H. *The Evolution of the Log House in Pioneer Ontario.* Paper presented at Log Structures in Canada conference, Ottawa, 1977.

Protecting Log Cabins from Decay (USDA Forest Services, Forest Products Laboratory, General Technical Report FPL-11). Madison, Wis.: U.S. Dept. of Agriculture Forest Service, Forest Products Laboratory, 1977. A small, first-rate pamphlet containing information on preventing logs from decay; prevents learning by trial and error.

Ramsey, Charles G., and Harold R. Sleeper. *Architectural Graphic Standards.* New York: John Wiley and Sons, 1970. Illustrates and details the exact methodology of modern construction. Very extensive load and stress tables, information on heavy timber construction. One of the most exhaustive and complete specifications books available to the designer. Expensive; not for beginners.

Rempel, John I., *Building with Wood.* Toronto, Ont.: University of Toronto Press, 1967. Well-researched and authoritative, this book provides very interesting reading on historical and aesthetic aspects of wood construction.

Roberts, Rex. *Your Engineered House.* New York: M. Evans and Company, 1964. A very personal book on functional design, especially on light, insulation and soundproofing your home.

Shurtleff, Harold R., *The Log Cabin Myth.* Gloucester, Mass.: Peter Smith, 1967. An interesting and well-documented book, written in 1939, whose major function is to prove that the Pilgrim forefathers of the United States did not live in log homes.

Sloane, Eric. *A Reverence for Wood.* New York: Random House, 1965. A lovingly done book, with beautiful illustrations, about how people used wood in the last century.

Stackwall: How to Build It. Northern Housing Committee. Winnipeg, Man.: University of Manitoba, 1977. A technical book on stackwall building produced as a result of the research into the subject by this Canadian university.

Walton, Harry. *Home and Workshop Guide to Sharpening.* New York: Harper and Row Publishers, Inc., 1967. Provides a well-illustrated and concise guide to this important aspect of woodworking.

Wass, Alonzo. *Building Construction Estimating.* Englewood Cliffs, N.J.: Prentice-Hall, Inc., 1970. A short manual of technical information for the professional and semi-professional builder.

Note: Figures in italics are illustrations.

authors

Dale Mann has been a professional log builder since 1973, first learning his craft by buying and reconstructing old log buildings in the Ottawa Valley of Ontario. Special features of his reconstructed buildings are their careful design, and the combination of antique and new architectural fittings and materials which maintain the quality and flavor of century-old buildings. In addition to his knowledge of carpentry and log building techniques, Dale Mann has a long-time interest in architecture and has travelled widely. He and his family divide their time between Toronto and the Ottawa Valley, where they have a log house on a cooperatively-owned farm.

Richard Skinulis has worked with Dale Mann in his log building business in southern and eastern Ontario. He has a background in journalism, and a special interest in the history of log building and rural life. Richard Skinulis now lives on a farm in Renfrew County, Ontario, in a geodesic dome which he built himself.

Nancy Shanoff is a commercial photographer presently doing freelance photography with Anzalone, McLeod, Stephens & Associates in Toronto, Ontario. Her clients include major advertising accounts, and her work has appeared in national magazines. Nancy Shanoff's fine color photographs contribute much to the appreciation of log houses in this, her first book.

Jane Nelson is a freelance illustrator who lives in Rockford, Illinois. Her fine work has appeared in magazines and newspapers, as well as on television. Jane Nelson has illustrated a number of books, notably *Chautauqua: A Center for Education, Religion and the Arts in America (1974)*.